Cambridge Elements ≡

Elements in Politics and Society in Latin America
edited by
Maria Victoria Murillo
Columbia University
Juan Pablo Luna
The Pontifical Catholic University of Chile
Tulia G. Falleti
University of Pennsylvania
Andrew Schrank
Brown University

T0286971

UNEVEN TRAJECTORIES

Latin American Societies in the Twenty-First Century

Gabriela Benza
National University of Tres de Febrero, Argentina
Gabriel Kessler
National University of General San Martín / National University of La Plata. Argentina

CAMBRIDGE
UNIVERSITY PRESS

CAMBRIDGE
UNIVERSITY PRESS

University Printing House, Cambridge CB2 8BS, United Kingdom

One Liberty Plaza, 20th Floor, New York, NY 10006, USA

477 Williamstown Road, Port Melbourne, VIC 3207, Australia

314–321, 3rd Floor, Plot 3, Splendor Forum, Jasola District Centre,
New Delhi – 110025, India

79 Anson Road, #06–04/06, Singapore 079906

Cambridge University Press is part of the University of Cambridge.

It furthers the University's mission by disseminating knowledge in the pursuit of
education, learning, and research at the highest international levels of excellence.

www.cambridge.org
Information on this title: www.cambridge.org/ 9781108745390
DOI: 10.1017/9781108775489

First published 2020

A catalogue record for this publication is available from the British Library.

ISBN 978-1-108-74539-0 Paperback
ISSN 2515-5245 (print)
ISSN 2515-5253 (online)

Uneven Trajectories

Latin American Societies in the Twenty-First Century

Elements in Politics and Society in Latin America

DOI: 10.1017/ 9781108775489
First published online: January 2020

Gabriela Benza
Gabriel Kessler
Author for correspondence: Gabriel Kessler, gabriel_kessler@yahoo.com.ar

Abstract: This Element presents the main characteristics of the current social structure in Latin America. We focus on demographic trends, migration, families, incomes, education, health and housing and examine the general policy trends for all of these issues. Our main questions are, What is the social structure in Latin America like today? What changes have taken place in recent decades, particularly since the turn of the millennium? We argue that although in some dimensions, there are continuities, including the persistence of problems from the past, we believe that the Latin American social structure, viewed as a whole, experienced significant transformations.

Keywords: Latin America, population, inequality, education, health, housing

ISBNs: (PB) 9781108745390 (OC) 9781108775489
ISSNs: 2515-5245 (print) 2515-5253 (online)

Contents

1 Introduction

The purpose of this Element is to present the main characteristics of the current social structure in Latin America. We focus on demographic trends, migration, families, incomes, education, health and housing, and we examine the general policy orientations for all of these issues. As such, we offer a comprehensive overview of common patterns in the social structure, as well as differences observed both between and within countries. Our study focuses on the new millennium, which has been referred to as 'post-neo-liberalism' or the 'Left Turn'. Between 1998 and 2011, centre-leftist or leftist presidents were indeed elected in eleven Latin American countries, but more generally we analyse the period of the economic boom that occurred in the region during the first decade of the twenty-first century.

Our main questions are, What is the social structure in Latin America like today? What changes have taken place in recent decades, particularly since the turn of the millennium? Are there common trends shared by different Latin American societies? The argument is that the economic boom and changes in public policies at the turn of the millennium increased the overall welfare of the population. However, Latin American societies continue to be structurally unequal in terms of class, gender and ethnicity. The improvement in welfare is the result of both public policies, such as conditional cash transfers, and a long-standing trend of reduced mortality and fertility, which started in the mid twentieth century. The growth in health and education coverage, as well as improvements in housing, had also contributed to the improvement of the welfare of the population, but new forms of inequality have emerged. In general terms, more than a decrease in inequalities, there was a decrease in the more extreme forms of exclusion.

How is Latin America today, compared to the past? Latin American society is more urban, enjoys greater longevity, receives more years of education and experiences less gender inequality than in the past. These changes, however, have taken place slowly but continuously over a period of time that began well before the post-neo-liberal period. Many of the trends began in the past, and some date back several decades. Demographic patterns and family relationships changed slowly, while transformations in health, education and housing were less sluggish because, although they are tied to demographic changes, they are also more sensitive to the policies of a given period. Some of these indicators had progressively begun to improve since the 1980s and 1990s. Overall, the trends of poverty and inequality in income and the labour market have been less stable because they are directly affected by changes in policy and economic cycles.

One might ask whether this means that transformation was only a matter of time and that the economic and political context of post-neo-liberalism did not leave its specific marks on the social structure. We argue that the post-neo-liberal period managed with relative success to achieve the unfulfilled promise of the social policies of the neo-liberal period: the creation of a basic safety net for the most excluded sectors. Indeed, what is particular to the post-neo-liberal period is, above all, improvements in the labour market and the increase in coverage of all kinds, particularly the extension of cash transfers through social policies as well as increased coverage of education, health and decent housing. On the other hand, significant inequalities remain, the rich became richer, and there were no major changes in the productive structure.

1.1 Why This Element?

Over the last decade, research has focused primarily on economic and political changes rather than transformations in the social structure as a whole. Although numerous studies and reports have been conducted on the different areas we discuss, limited resources are available offering the kind of comprehensive overview which we aim to offer with this Element. We believe this goal to be particularly relevant given that the aforementioned political and economic cycle has come to a close. Economic growth and the commodities boom have given rise to an uncertain economic situation, and the Pink Tide has been followed by a heterogeneous state of affairs marked by turns to the right and centre right, but also to the left, as occurred in Mexico in 2018. An updated understanding of Latin American society is fundamental for considering the political and social processes taking place in the region today.

We have chosen to analyse the most central aspects of societies in the region. First, the Element reviews demographic issues, such as spatial distribution of the population, age, trends in mortality and fertility, processes of urbanisation, family relations and migrations. Demographic processes have a great impact on individual life trajectories and on social dynamics, and they entail specific challenges for socio-economic development. They are also key variables to be considered in policy planning. Indeed, the challenges for socio-economic development and public policy in areas like health care, education and housing clearly differ in contexts marked by high birth and death rates or by intense migration processes. Second, we address the population's income distribution. This section is organised around a central debate of the post-neo-liberal period: has there been a real decrease in income inequality? We describe changes in income for different social classes and the variables involved when considering the structural limitations on lowering inequality. Finally, we conclude our analysis by reviewing three key areas related to the population's well-being: education, health and housing. We present general trends, changes that have taken place, new and old problems and the main policies of the period.

1.2 Latin America in the New Millennium

During the 1980s and 1990s, prior to this Element's period of focus, a wave of neo-liberal reform swept across Latin America in the context of the debt crisis and structural adjustment policies promoted by multilateral organisations like the International Monetary Fund and World Bank. According to Huber and Stephens (2012, 156), neo-liberal leaders 'diagnose the roots of the crisis as excessive state intervention in markets and fiscal irresponsibility' and therefore recommend the 'reduction of government expenditures, liberalisation of trade and financial markets, privatisation and deregulation as remedies. In the area of social policy, the prescriptions were partial or full privatisation of social security, increasing reliance on private providers and market principles in health care and education, and targeting of the state's provision of transfers and the neediest groups'.

With regard to the true scope of these neo-liberal reforms, results were mixed. Some policies intended to bring flexibility to the labour market affected at least 10 countries as well as social security reforms aimed at mixed or private systems in eleven countries (Lora, 2007). But there were no radical transformations in education and housing, and, in the case of health, systemic changes only took place in Chile and Colombia. We agree with Cortés and Marshall (1999) that neo-liberal reform had its greatest impact in areas that, like labour and social security, were central to achieving economic reform and increasing capital gains. However, the period of neo-liberal reform was shorter than that imagined by its proponents, and, following the leftward shift, a large portion of the ambitious programme of reforms was left incomplete.

We can now turn to the question of the status of Latin American society following the neo-liberal decade. Data show a rise in inequality and varying results with regard to poverty. In its 1999 report, the Economic Commission for Latin America and the Caribbean (ECLAC, 2002) stated that 211 million people, 43.8 per cent of the Latin American population, were poor. In 1980, the figure had been 40.5 per cent, or 135.9 million poor people, and in 1990, 48.3 per cent, or more than 200 million. In the 1990s, there was a relative reduction in the population living in poverty with differences between countries, but there was a parallel rise in the absolute population living below the poverty line due to demographic growth. In other words, the percentage was lower, but a greater overall number of people were living in poverty because the population itself had grown.

While the evolution of poverty figures showed differences between countries, inequality rose in nearly all of them. The same ECLAC report showed that between 1990 and 1999, the Gini coefficient on income inequality increased or remained the same in most countries, with very high values in thirteen countries, and only decreased by a small margin in three. With regard to the indicator for relative poverty, that is, the segment of the population with a per capita income of less than 50 per cent of the average, only two of the sixteen countries considered by ECLAC showed a reduction; in the rest, this indicator rose, and the outlook at the end of the decade was pessimistic. After 1990, the rate of informal employment also grew by 5 percentage points, or more than 20 million people, and the urban unemployment rate climbed from 5.5 per cent in 1990 to 10.8 per cent in 1999, particularly in South America. Social spending grew during this decade by 50 per cent, from an average of $360 per capita in 1990 to $540 at the end of the decade.

The so-called neo-liberal period was followed by the Left Turn. As mentioned above, between 1998 and 2011, leftist presidents were elected in eleven different Latin American countries. According to Roberts (2012), two-thirds of the regional population was under the authority of leftist national governments. Beyond differences between countries, this change led to the introduction of redistribution policies through both social and labour legislation. However, as we shall see in the second section, some of these policies were also adopted by centre-right and right-wing governments. The Left Turn coincided with a period of rapid and sustained economic growth. In a favourable international context, economic growth was accompanied by improvements in the labour market and income distribution, as well as a decrease in poverty, at least until 2012. Beccaria (2016) gives an overview of trends during the period, stating that a large number of countries experienced economic expansion after 2003: between that year and 2011, the average rate of growth in gross domestic product (GDP) reached 4.4 per cent annually. This trend continued during the first years of the 2010s, although with lower rates in 2012 and 2013 (2.9 per cent each year) and a marked deceleration since then. Beccaria emphasises that this was a nearly unprecedented level of growth tied to advancements in the international context and more appropriate management of macroeconomic policy.

Economic expansion had a positive impact on job creation and the evolution of the employment rate. According to ECLAC data, open unemployment dropped from 11.4 per cent in 2002 to 6.9 per cent in 2014. Formal jobs, that is, those registered with social security, increased. However, nearly half of employed individuals do not have social security coverage. Wages have risen since 2003, especially in South America. The Gini coefficient of family income inequality was reduced from 0.547 in 2002 to 0.491 in 2014, while the percentage of people living below the poverty line fell from 43.9 per cent to 28.2 per cent between the same years. However, since 2012 and with the change in the international situation, improvements have tended to slow, and even to stagnate.

The Left Turn and the commodities boom are over. This Element aims to contribute to the debate on the period that has just ended in order to create an assessment of the status of societies and social structures. In the first section, we shall review demographic trends in mortality and fertility, spatial distribution of the population, migrations and families. In the second section, we will focus on the central question of the period, regarding the decrease in inequality and the related economic, social and political factors. We will review trends in inequality and their limitations, considering what has occurred in different social classes and with regard to labour. In the third section, we will concentrate on education, health and housing conditions for the population, and on state actions. In the conclusion, we will go back to this Element's argument and shall try to provide a response to the question of what has changed in Latin American societies.

This Element is based mainly on data and statistical reports that consider global trends in Latin America and depends also on available Caribbean data. Among our main sources are reports by international organisations such as ECLAC, the Inter-American Development Bank (IDB) and the Pan American Health Organization (PAHO) as well as research from different countries and diverse data sources.

2 Population

Our focus in this section is the structure and dynamics of the population in Latin America. We first examine the evolution of the population size, death rates and birth rates. Then we focus on the transformations in families, and finally, we turn to the spatial distribution of the population and to internal and external migration. During this millennium, there have been significant changes in demographic dynamics, families and urbanisation. These changes were initiated or accelerated during the second half of the twentieth century. In fact, demographic changes are slower, and turning points do not necessarily coincide with specific economic and political contexts. The fall in the mortality and fertility rates brought an increase in the well-being of the population. However, long-lasting problems of inequality between countries and social groups persist.

2.1 The Demographic Transition

Approximately 624 million people, or 8.5 per cent of the world's population, live in Latin America, according to United Nations data from 2015 (UN DESA, 2019). Distribution varies greatly between different countries. More than half of the region's population is concentrated in Brazil (more than 200 million inhabitants) and Mexico (more than 120 million), while other countries, such as Uruguay, Panama and Costa Rica, are home to no more than 5 million inhabitants each (Figure 1).

The population of Latin America has been increasing at progressively lower rates, after intense growth in the mid twentieth century. During those years, the region had the world's highest rates of population expansion, sparking concern and debates about the negative effects this demographic explosion would have on opportunities for economic development (CELADE-UNFPA, 2005). After peaking at 2.7 per cent for the period of 1960–5, however, the annual population growth rate in Latin America began to wane. It currently stands at 1.1 per cent, according to data from 2010 to 2015, and it is estimated that it will drop to nearly zero (approximately 0.02 per cent) by 2055–60 (UN DESA, 2019). In any case, today, population growth in Latin America remains high when compared to growth in developed regions, with important differences between countries: Cuba and Uruguay, for example, have extremely low rates, at 0.2 per cent and 0.3 per cent, respectively, while Guatemala is experiencing a significant rise with a rate of 2.1 per cent.

The evolution of population size over time is closely tied to the demographic transition, a process of social change characterised by a reduction in mortality and fertility rates. In Latin America, this transition did not begin until the twentieth century, much later than in developed countries. However, it was also much more rapid. If the region is viewed as a whole, the period of rapid population growth in the middle of the last century marked the initial stage of the transition, when a decline in mortality began in many countries but fertility rates remained high. Later, when these rates began to drop, the pace of population expansion also slowed.

However, the demographic transition has different timing and intensity. ECLAC (2008) has classified LAC countries into four stages of demographic transition according to total fertility rates and life expectancy: very advanced, advanced, full and moderate. For example, Argentina and Uruguay are in an advanced or very advanced stage. They experienced early transitions with substantial reductions in fertility and mortality during the first half of the twentieth century. Cuba, Brazil, Chile, Colombia, Costa Rica and Mexico began the transition a couple decades later but at a very intense pace. In contrast,

Figure 1 Latin America and the Caribbean: total population by subregion and country, 2015 (millions).

Source: UN DESA(2019)

Bolivia, Guatemala and Haiti are in the moderate transition stage: the drop in mortality and fertility occurred later and at a slower rate.

2.2 Fertility and Life Expectancy

After the turn of the century, mortality and fertility continued to decline, although at a slower pace in countries in very advanced or advanced stages of the demographic transition. From a long-term perspective, these demographic trends have radically changed the life experiences of the region's inhabitants. The reduction in mortality has allowed for a significant increase in life expectancy at birth, which rose from 51.4 years in 1950–5 to 74.4 years in 2010–15. During this time, the difference between Latin America and more developed regions diminished considerably. While Latin Americans in the mid twentieth century expected to live twelve years less than Europeans and seventeen years less than Americans and Canadians, the difference has now been reduced to three and five years, respectively (UN DESA, 2019). However, although the extension of life expectancy has reached all countries in the region, inequalities persist (Figure 2). In fact, the life expectancy at birth in Puerto Rico and Costa Rica stands at seventy-nine years and in Cuba and Chile at seventy-eight, but it is only sixty-one in Haiti and sixty-nine in Bolivia. In other words, life expectancy varies by up to eighteen years depending on the country one inhabits.

Improvement in the population's living conditions, advances in medicine and expanded health care systems have all contributed to increased life expectancy. The reduction of the infant mortality rate has made a significant contribution to this process, plummeting from 126 deaths of infants under one year old per 1000 live births in the mid twentieth century to 17 per 1000 live births in the period 2010–15 (UN DESA, 2019). This decrease, which applies to all countries and has remained constant over time, can mainly be attributed to the decreasing incidence of deaths from parasitic and bacterial respiratory infections that inordinately affect children (Chackiel, 2004).

As occurs in most modern societies, the drop in mortality rates has been stronger in women than in men, further exacerbating the gender gap in life

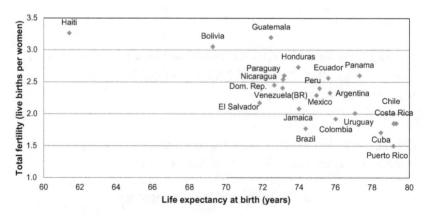

Figure 2 Latin America and the Caribbean: total fertility and life expectancy at birth by country, 2010–15.

Source: UN DESA (2019)

expectancy at birth: from 1950–5 to 2010–15, women's life expectancy rose fifty-three years, to the age of seventy-eight, while that of men increased by fifty years, to seventy-one (UN DESA, 2019). This difference is connected to a lower rate of death from causes that affect women more than men, such as those associated with reproductive health and complications from pregnancy and childbirth. In contrast, the decrease in the causes of death more frequent among men, such as those associated with cardiovascular diseases and external causes (violence, accidents and traumatism), has been less marked.

The drop in fertility was rapid and sustained, even though it began later than the decline in mortality rates. While the total fertility rate for the region was 5.8 children per woman in 1950–5, by 2010–15, it had fallen to the replacement level, that is, the minimum fertility rate for a closed population (i.e. not counting migrations) to hold steady over time, of 2.1 children per woman (UN DESA, 2019). The trend has been so intense that it has surpassed estimates made for the region at different points in time. As a result, Latin America went from having one of the world's highest reproductive rates to having rates below the global average (2.5 children per women), even if they are always higher than in Europe (1.6) and North America (1.8).

The reduction in fertility rates is associated with changes in reproductive preferences and especially with a continuous reduction in the number of children women hope to have, as revealed in surveys that date back to the 1960s. The exercise of reproductive rights, i.e. having the number of children one wants to have, was made possible – albeit, as we will see, with certain limitations – thanks to the birth control revolution, which can be attributed to biotechnology (increased production and more reliable contraceptive methods), policies (family planning programmes) and cultural shifts (greater social acceptance of the use of contraceptives) (CELADE-UNFPA, 2005).

Evidence shows that, in this process, differences in fertility rates between countries and between women from different social sectors were reduced. However, disparities persist. There are currently countries in the region where the total fertility rate is below the replacement level, such as Cuba, Uruguay, Chile, Colombia, Costa Rica and Brazil. Yet other countries, such as Bolivia and Guatemala, are still at more than one child above the replacement level (Figure 2). On the other hand, the gaps between social classes remain important. Data for Bolivia, Colombia, Haiti, Honduras, Peru and the Dominican Republic show that the total fertility rate of women in the lowest income quintile is between 2 and 3 times higher than that of women in the highest one (Rodríguez Vignoli, 2014).

The decrease in fertility rates was not accompanied by a sustained rise in the maternity age. In aggregate terms, there is no evidence of a substantial postponement of the start of a woman's reproductive life (Cabella and Pardo, 2014). However, this trend seems to be the result of different behaviours according to socio-economic status (SES): middle- and upper-class women tend to increasingly put off motherhood, while poorer women continue to have children at around the same age. According to UN Women (2017) data, by 2010, the percentage of women who had already been a mother at age nineteen was only 6 per cent among those with a high educational level (thirteen or more years of instruction) but amounted to 59 per cent among those with a low educational level (five to eight years of instruction).

Closely related to the aforementioned is that there hasn't been a great change in adolescent fertility rates, which have remained high. Adolescent fertility is concentrated mainly among women of lower SES and is particularly high among indigenous women (see Figure 3). The persistence of high adolescent fertility rates is a particularly significant issue because of its normative and social implications. Latin America has been considered something of an 'anomaly' worldwide (Rodríguez Vignoli, Di Cesare and Páez, 2017) because it is far above the global average with regard to adolescent birth rates, surpassed only by sub-Saharan Africa. These levels are much higher than what would be expected given the overall fertility rate and other social indicators, such as educational attainment levels and the degree of urbanisation. Yet although adolescent

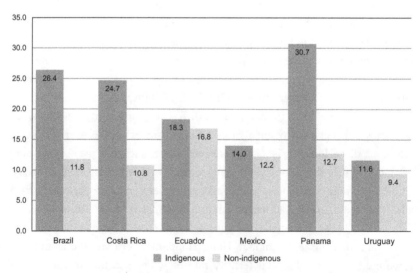

Figure 3 Latin America (nine countries): percentages of adolescent women (aged fifteen to nineteen years) who are mothers according to ethnic condition, circa 2010.

Source: ECLAC (2013)

fertility rates remain high, they have dropped slightly since the beginning of the twenty-first century, making it possible to posit that a change in this trend may be under way (Rodríguez Vignoli, 2014).

2.3 Consequences of Mortality and Fertility Trends

The reduction in fertility and mortality has modified the age structure of Latin America's population. The proportion of children (ages 0–14) has dropped since the 1970s, due in part to dwindling fertility rates. In addition, the proportion of adults (ages fifteen to fifty-nine) has risen, especially the number of elderly people (ages sixty and older), in a trend that is expected to continue (Figure 4).

The change in the population's age structure has had important consequences. The first is the modification in the dependency ratio, i.e. the number of individuals typically in the workforce (ages fifteen to fifty-nine) versus those typically not in the workforce (ages zero to fourteen and sixty and older). Shifting age structures can create imbalances between the resources of working-age people, for whom labour income typically exceeds consumption, and the young and old, who often produce less than they consume. However, the magnitude of these imbalances and the ages at which people really earn more through their labour than they consume vary greatly depending on economic conditions and public policy (see National Transfer Accounts in Lee and Mason, 2006).

In Latin America, at the start of the demographic transition and until the middle of the twentieth century, the dependency ratio was high because the reduction in child mortality, combined with persistently high fertility rates, led to a particularly large child population. The growing demand for places at

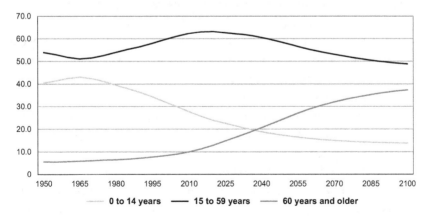

Figure 4 Latin America and the Caribbean: percentage of population by broad age group, 1950–2100.

Source: UN DESA (2019)

schools posed challenges for education systems. Later, as fertility rates dropped, the dependency ratio also began to diminish since the child population began to fall, and the elderly population had not yet risen significantly.

The favourable balance between the typically active and inactive population has led to the notion of Latin America currently experiencing a 'demographic window of opportunity' conducive to economic development. Society has an abundant workforce to stimulate the economy, and a more numerous population of working-age individuals can make greater contributions to social security and pension systems. At the same time, a reduced child population alleviates pressure on education systems. Finally, in lower-income homes, the proportion of those needing care in each household falls, while the proportion of those able to work rises, thus increasing opportunities to escape from poverty.

However, there is no guarantee of the benefits associated with the demographic window, as these depend on the implementation of macroeconomic policies that encourage investment in production and increase the economy's potential to create jobs. Without such policies, the benefits of the window are lost, and the lack of job opportunities for a population with many working-age individuals poses its own problems. Investments in education and training for youth are also crucial. The experience of the so-called Asian Tigers is telling in this regard. These countries, particularly South Korea, seized the demographic window to drive economic growth by making solid investments in education. In Latin America, however, there have been no policies in recent decades aimed at making the most of the demographic window of opportunity, which will eventually close. According to recent projections, it will end in the region around 2027, earlier than estimated in previous demographic studies, though with significant variations between countries (ECLAC, 2015a).

The end of the demographic window is linked to population ageing, the second particularly important consequence of the mortality and fertility trends discussed above. The percentage of elderly adults in the region is growing significantly: while 5.6 per cent of the total population was elderly in 1950, the percentage currently stands at 11.4 per cent (UN DESA, 2019). This tendency is expected to continue, and by 2040, the elderly population will surpass the child population.

As in other regions, the process of population ageing stands out because among the elderly, there is an increasing number of the oldest members due to increased life expectancy; in other words, the region is home to a rising number of individuals who are likely to require special care. The elderly population is also predominantly female due to the fact that women's life expectancy is greater. A large number of these women are widows who spend the last years of their lives alone, often lacking the income necessary to cover their basic needs.

Yet despite the inexorable process of population ageing, Latin America is still far removed from the situation currently faced by other regions. The percentage of the elderly population in Latin America is currently very similar to that of Europe in 1950. Today, Europe is the region with the highest levels of population ageing (23.8 per cent). Within Latin America, the situation differs from country to country: the proportion of elderly residents is very high in Uruguay (19.2 per cent), a country that experienced an early transition, but also in Cuba (19.4 per cent) due to the very rapid reduction of fertility and increase in life expectancy this country has experienced since the mid twentieth century. In contrast, in countries in less advanced stages in demographic transition, a lower percentage of the population is elderly. This is the case in Guatemala (6.7 per cent), Honduras (6.5 per cent) and Haiti (7.1 per cent) (UN DESA, 2019).

Demographic ageing brings important social challenges. First, it creates a need to re-examine the way elderly people are viewed, the role they play and their contributions to society. Contrary to other regions, this population group in Latin America is still often seen as fragile, dependent and vulnerable. However, the elderly represents a highly heterogeneous group, and as Lloyd-Sherlock (2000) notes, this is particularly so in developing nations like those of Latin America due to social inequalities. The experience of old age has notable variations depending on one's social class, which affects the number of years a person can expect to live and the conditions of this stage of life (physical abilities, autonomous living, material living standards and the possibility of receiving the care one requires).

In terms of public policy, population ageing is an issue that must be addressed, among other reasons, due to the high level of care the elderly often require. In Latin American societies, these activities have traditionally been relegated to the private sphere and families. Women – daughters or, in some cases, daughters-in-law – are overwhelmingly the caregivers of the elderly. As part of demographic ageing, generations of women are now spending more years looking after their parents or the parents of their spouses than their own children. A greater demand for care, however, takes place within a context of growing autonomy for women and changes in household organisation. Nonetheless, only the highest income groups can pay for caregivers to look after their elderly family members. It is therefore of pressing importance for the region to create specific public policies to address these issues. Such policies have so far, however, been scarce on the agendas of Latin American governments.

Population ageing also creates new and greater demands for the traditional institutions entrusted with public well-being, which now must guarantee health care and economic security for the elderly population. Although Latin American health care systems are not yet dealing with the numbers of elderly adults seen in regions such as Europe, it seems necessary for them to begin reorienting services to the needs of this population group and its specific epidemiological profiles. Similarly, the increase in the inactive population poses a challenge for social security systems. First, in terms of sustainability, this is a problem the region shares with developed countries. Additionally, however, Latin American countries face a problem in terms of ageing that is related to their labour markets. Many elderly Latin Americans do not qualify for social security due to unstable labour trajectories and the prevalence of informal work, meaning that countries must come up with novel ways to guarantee these individuals a certain level of material well-being.

Finally, fertility trends in the region also entail specific concerns for public policy. In Latin America, policies related to fertility initially received attention in the mid twentieth century. At that time, the focus was on keeping the birth rate under control, as rapid demographic growth was viewed as an obstacle to economic development. This perspective, highly controversial even at the time, eventually led to a paradigm shift and new visions in which people were treated as subjects of rights. As part of this new paradigm, policies related to fertility began to focus on the right to sexual and reproductive health, to freely decide on the number of children individuals would have and when they would have them and on women's autonomy.

Already exceeding estimates, the reduction in the region's fertility rate should lay to rest arguments for the necessity of population control. Yet these trends also pose problems for policies that seek to guarantee women's sexual and reproductive rights. One particular issue is the dualistic structure of reproductive behaviours observed in countries in the region. This dualism, an expression of profound social inequalities, requires policies that do not merely address population averages (Pardo & Varela, 2013). For example, among low-SES women and particularly adolescents in this group, undesired pregnancies are a major problem. In this case, it appears that specific sexual and reproductive health care policies are needed, different from those that have been successful among other age groups (Rodríguez Vignoli, 2014). In general, it is possible that in the near future, women who have fewer children and are already postponing motherhood, as well as challenging the traditional ideas about it, pose an entirely different challenge for public policy. It will be necessary to ensure that these women, if they wish to do so, are able to have children through policies that provide flexibility for managing both work and family (Pardo & Varela, 2013).

Finally, in the struggle to guarantee the sexual and reproductive rights of women, it is essential to consider the status of abortion in the region. There are only four countries – Cuba, Guyana, Puerto Rico and Uruguay – where abortion is allowed with no legal restrictions of any kind, according to 2018 data. In the other countries in the region, laws are restrictive, and in six countries, abortion is entirely prohibited. The vast majority of abortions in the region are therefore unsafe. Often carried out by individuals who lack medical training and/or at centres that do not meet minimal medical standards, abortion causes high rates of maternal mortality and morbidity. At least 10 per cent of the total maternal deaths in the region are due to unsafe abortions, and about 760 000 women are treated annually for complications arising from these practices (Guttmacher Institute, 2018). Once again, social differences also come into play here, as poor women are more likely to suffer the complications associated with unsafe abortions.

2.4 Transformations in Families

Families in Latin America have undergone significant changes as to their structures and dynamics due to the demographic trends discussed above, but also because of other social, economic and cultural processes. These changes became noticeable during the final decades of the twentieth century and have led to greater diversity in family living arrangements.

For instance, consensual unions have gained ground in comparison to legal marriages, and rates of separation and divorce have gone up. Consensual unions in particular have shown strong and generalised growth, though often as a 'trial' period before a possible marriage. The 'cohabitation boom' (Esteve & Lesthaeghe, 2016) has occurred both in countries in which entering that type of union was already very common (as in Central America and the Caribbean) and in those where it was less frequent (such as Argentina, Brazil or Chile). Esteve and Lesthaeghe (2016) show, for example, that the percentage of consensual unions in the Dominican Republic, historically very high, rose from 60.8 per cent in 1980 to 78.4 per cent in 2010 among partnered women between twenty-five and twenty-nine years of age, while in Argentina that percentage increased five-fold from a low 13.0 per cent to 65.5 per cent during the same period. These rates are much higher than those observed in many developed countries.

Transformations in the trends of forming and dissolving families have been seen by some as part of a second demographic transition driven by changes in the preferences and values of the population: the search for personal fulfilment instead of family projects and commitments, along with greater autonomy for women leading to an increased ability to end unsatisfactory marriages. However, this view has also been nuanced. Consensual unions are far from novel in Latin America, especially in regions with large indigenous and Afro–Latin American populations. This has historically been the form of union most broadly entered into among low-income groups, tied to cultural heritage and lower economic costs. Therefore, this should not necessarily be interpreted as the expression of new trends towards reduced adhesion to institutional controls, although it is true that in recent decades its frequency has raised, and it has become an increasingly common option for the middle and upper classes. Moreover, the subordination of women continues to be a serious problem, and it may be the case that separations and divorces do not lead to greater autonomy for women but rather just the opposite, particularly in cases in which women must take on the economic support and care of their children alone.

Other conditions related to the formation of families have been more resistant to change, most notably when compared to trends in the US or Western Europe. This is especially true with regard to the ages at which relevant transitions are made. On the one hand, the age at entering into a union, which falls between those observed in developed countries and countries in Asia and Africa, has remained relatively stable (Spijker, López Ruiz & Palós, 2012). Although there has been evidence in recent years of this step being delayed, the trend seems to be due mainly to changes in the behaviours of the middle and upper classes; among lower classes, the pattern of forming a family early continues (Cerrutti & Binstock, 2009). On the other hand, as we have seen, the age at which women have their first child seems to follow a similar pattern: on the average, there has not been significant change, although women at a higher socio-economic level do seem to be having children later.

The size and make-up of households show some transformations. Households in the region are now smaller than in the past, given the drop on fertility and the increase in people living alone (due mainly to population aging, as well as separations and divorces and a greater number of young people, especially from the middle and upper classes, living alone). While in 1990 the average size of households in the region was 4.2 people, by 2010 that number had dropped to 3.5. There has also been an increase in the diversity of types of households. Traditional households, made up of a conjugal union with children, are still the most common (40.3 per cent in 2010) and that extended families, in which other family members live together, always also have a considerable presence (19 per cent), in many cases due to a lack of housing and economic hardship. However, other types of households have become more common in practically all countries: first, single-person households increased from 7.0 per cent to 11.4 per cent between 1990 and 2010; second, the proportion of single-parent households, made up of a mother or father and their children, rose from 9.1 per cent to 12.4 per cent during the same period (Ullman, Maldonado Valera & Rico, 2014). In both cases, the presence of women is very important. Single-person households are mainly formed by elderly women, due to their greater life expectancy and widowhood. Single-parent homes are primarily made up of women who, after a separation or divorce, live with their children. This latter group has been the object of special attention because of a very high incidence of poverty.

Within countries, transformations in the size and make-up of households have not had the same intensity across different sectors of society. Lower-income households, in the lowest quintile, are still much more numerous than those with higher incomes in the top quintile (4.5 people vs. 2.7, on the average). Two-parent households with children and extended family households were, and are, more common among lower-income classes. And while the increase in single-mother arrangements has been especially typical in lower-income households, that of single-person households has been greater among more privileged classes (Ullman, Maldonado Valera & Rico, 2014; Rico & Maldonado Valera, 2011). There is also still significant heterogeneity among countries, according to their stage in the demographic transition and their level of socio-economic development, as shown by Ariza and de Oliveira (2008).

But there have been more modifications to family living arrangements than those discussed here. There is evidence of a greater incidence of other family types not covered by surveys (Cienfuegos, 2014). First are multi-local or transnational families due to migration: family units separated by geographical distances but tightly knit through material and symbolic exchanges that guarantee their day-to-day continuity. Next are families with same-sex parents, on which data are vague given that not all censuses recognise their existence. It is possible that these families have expanded in the new millennium due to a less hostile social context and the passing of laws in several Latin American countries that allow same-sex marriage. Finally, we come to blended families, the product of new unions after separations or divorces, which in statistics tend to be included with traditional two-parent nuclear households. In short, change also involves a greater presence of families that, until now, have not been visible in the region's statistical systems.

In the sphere of family dynamics and particularly in that of gender relations between family members, there are new trends and also significant continuities. Women in Latin America have been increasing their participation in the labour market since the 1970s, with their practices becoming more and more similar to those of men. As a result, there has been an increase in two-parent two-breadwinner households, in which both partners work outside the home.

There has been a reduction in those that follow the traditional division of work by gender with a male breadwinner and female housewife. However, this change has not come hand in hand with an equivalent one regarding equality in housework and childcare. Studies based on surveys regarding use of time coincide in all cases: women spend more time than their partners on household chores and childcare, even in cases in which both partners participate in the labour market. On average, Latin American women spend 3 times more time on domestic work than men (37.9 vs. 12.7 hours per week, respectively). And while among women the burden of unpaid domestic work varies significantly according to their age, geographic location, type of activity, economic and family situation, among men the variations are much smaller: participation is always limited in all social class. This persistence of traditional gender roles occurs in the context of large gaps in coverage and failures in the quality of childcare, leading to a greater workload for women and increased difficulties for their incorporation in the labour market.

2.5 Spatial Distribution and Population Mobility

The population of Latin America is distributed unequally not only between countries but also within them. In fact, the nations of Latin America are distinguished by the spatial concentration of their populations in urban areas and within such areas, in large cities. The percentage of city inhabitants is, according to United Nations data from 2015 (UN DESA, 2018), almost 80 per cent, just slightly below the rate in North America (82 per cent) and much higher than the world average (54 per cent) (Figure 5). Some of the world's largest cities are found in Latin America, including four megalopolises (cities with 10 million inhabitants or more): San Pablo and Rio de Janeiro in Brazil, Mexico City and Buenos Aires, Argentina.

Urban life in the region dates back centuries. The main indigenous groups lived in large cities, and during the conquest, urban centres formed the foundation for the material and symbolic power cultivated by the Spaniards (Rodríguez Vignoli, 2002). However, the highly urban character of Latin America today is mainly a product of the twentieth century. One of the main demographic trends of the past century has been the rapid transformation of a predominantly rural region to an overwhelmingly urban one.

In 1925, only a quarter of Latin America's population lived in urban areas (Lattes, Rodríguez & Villa, 2003). Since then, cities have expanded at a dizzying rate, with Latin America's urban population rising from 41.3 per cent in 1950 to 57.3 per cent in 1970. This growth, which was concentrated in just a few cities in each country, garnered worldwide notice

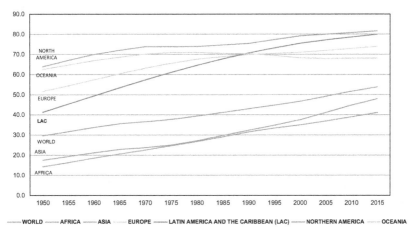

Figure 5 Percentage of population residing in urban areas by region, 1950–2015.

Source: UN DESA (2018)

and led to the consolidation of urban systems that were structured around large-scale cities that tend to be highly primate.

During the period of intense urbanisation, the main factor in the expansion of cities was mass migration from the countryside. The modernisation of rural production, which diminished the need for field hands, combined with a lack of access to land, led a growing number of rural dwellers to migrate to cities. Generally, these migrants were working-age youth with limited economic resources and little education.

The industrialisation taking place in the region also fomented this population flow towards cities. For many of these migrants, industrial jobs provided a clear opportunity for social mobility, particularly in countries with more pronounced industrial development. However, rural–urban migration in Latin America was less connected to economic and social progress than it was in developed countries (ECLAC, 2014a). A considerable group of migrants felt obliged to leave their birthplaces rather than being attracted by real opportunities offered by cities. In general, Latin America's economies were unable to create enough jobs for this massive group of migrants, and many were forced to accept low-skill jobs within the growing informal sector. The state did not provide adequate services or housing for migrants, who overwhelmingly formed part of marginalised groups relegated to precarious settlements that would later become slums on the city's outskirts.

The process of urbanisation declined during the last decades of the twentieth century, and it is currently expected to continue, though at a slower pace. While during the period of rapid urban expansion, which lasted until the 1970s, the growth rate of cities stood at around 4 per cent per year, it gradually began to fall, reaching approximately 1.5 per cent in 2015.

The deceleration of urban growth may help alleviate associated problems, such as the lack of basic services and housing. However, the intensity of urbanisation – and related issues – varies among the countries in Latin America. Some countries have high levels of urban growth, with 85 per cent or more of the population living in cities. This is the case in Argentina, Chile and Uruguay, where the process began early and the urban population surpassed the rural population in the 1930s, and in Venezuela and Brazil, where urbanisation began later but at a rapid pace. In other countries, such as Haiti, Guatemala, Honduras, Nicaragua, Jamaica and Paraguay, urban growth remains low (under 60 per cent), and though the number of people living in cities is increasing, the rates vary.

The main factor that explains the diminished expansion of cities in the region is the gradual reduction of rural–urban migration. While this migration was the predominant flow among the Latin American population for decades, it now plays a more minor role: during the 1950s, 46 per cent of urban growth was attributed to rural–urban flows, while this percentage fell to 38 per cent between 1990 and 2000 (Lattes, Rodríguez & Villa, 2003). However, people continue to abandon the Latin American countryside. In fact, if Latin America's migration to cities had not continued, the region would have ruralised due to the higher natural growth, i.e. the difference between the number of live births and the number of deaths, that continues among rural dwellers (ECLAC, 2012).

The reduction of rural–urban flows has been accompanied by an increase of migration between cities to the point where today's migration flows are predominantly urban-urban. The flows between cities, however, are more complex and difficult to measure and appear to have a great degree of internal diversity.

As in the case of the traditional rural–urban flow, part of this migration is due to some cities' sluggish labour market and/or high poverty rates, leading migrants to move to cities with more dynamic economies and job markets. Yet, as noted by Rodríguez Vignoli (2011) in an analysis of 2000 census data, not all urban–urban migration fits this description. In addition to economic and labour factors, there are others, such as communication advantages, location, quality of life, lower levels of violence and insecurity (whether real or perceived), less contamination and lower living costs.

On the other hand, the relationship between migration and city size varies greatly between countries, though certain trends can be detected. The most noteworthy feature of this migration is the outward flow from small cities, with a negative migration rate in comparison to the rest of the cities of the urban system. At the same time, cities of 5 million inhabitants or more seem to have lost their historical appeal: in general terms, their growth is below average, and net emigration has become the norm. This trend, however, does not apply to large cities of more than 1 million inhabitants (Rodríguez Vignoli, 2011). Another significant trend is intra-metropolitan moves. A significant portion of migration is small scale, that is, within the same city, with flows usually moving from the centre towards the periphery (Cerrutti & Bertoncello, 2006). These movements reflect the consolidation of long-term processes – principally, the difficulties of living in a city's downtown area, mainly faced by the poor – along with more recent phenomena, such as the suburbanisation of wealthier groups.

Finally, urban–urban migration seems to involve population groups with different socio-economic profiles than those of traditional rural–urban migrants. These new migrant groups do not necessarily have a lower level of education or a lower SES than the resident population. Migrants and residents seem to have more similar socio-demographic features (Cerrutti & Bertoncello, 2006), a result that can be at least partially attributed to the significant expansion of educational coverage and the reduction of social gaps in education access, as we shall discuss further on, in the past few decades in Latin America.

Migratory trends and the specific nature of natural growth in different urban areas have brought about changes to the region's urban systems. Since the last decades of the twentieth century, there has been a reduction in the growth rate of large cities in countries with high primacy. At the same time, the importance of intermediate cities has increased. The demographic growth of these cities has been quite dynamic, though the population in such cities remains lower than it is in developed countries (UN-Habitat, 2012).

2.6 International Migrations

Population movements to foreign countries have historically been a central demographic feature in Latin America and continue to be significant today. The region once attracted a great number of overseas immigrants, particularly from Europe, in addition to continuous movements between Latin American regions. However, beginning in the mid twentieth century, Latin America became a sending region, and since then, it has had a negative net migration rate. As a result, the total growth of the population has been slightly less than the natural increase.

An estimated 28.5 million Latin Americans, or 4.8 per cent of the region's total population, were living outside their countries of birth in 2010. The number of emigrant populations varies considerably from country to country but is very high in Central America and the Caribbean. In Jamaica and El

Salvador, the percentage of citizens living abroad is 29.3 per cent and 21.8 per cent, respectively, while in Nicaragua, Cuba, Haiti and the Dominican Republic, this percentage stands at around 10 per cent (Martínez Pizarro & Orrego Rivera, 2016). The case of Mexico merits particular attention since it is the country with the highest number of emigrants (nearly 12 million people) not only in the region but also worldwide. In addition, it is also a country of transit for thousands of people from other countries travelling to the US.

Once of the most visible expressions of the importance of emigration in Latin America is the quantity of remittances. Money transfers sent home to family members by emigrants have grown significantly since the 1990s, and currently they constitute an important economic contribution to numerous countries in the region. In 2015, remittances totalled approximately US$65.6 billion, or 1.3 per cent of the region's GDP. For the economies of certain countries, especially in the Caribbean and Central America, remittances are even more significant. In Haiti, Jamaica, Honduras and El Salvador, money sent from abroad represents more than 15 per cent of GDP (CEMLA, 2016). Remittances play a key role in maintaining many families, and evidences for some countries, such as Mexico, indicates that they work as a channel to reduce poverty and inequality, since lower-income households are more likely to receive them (Beaton et al., 2017).

Limited life opportunities, political and social conflicts and human rights violations have all contributed to successive waves of Latin American emigration. The main destination has been the US, which has received large numbers of people from Mexico and the Caribbean, followed by a number of emigrants from Central and South American nations. A total of 20 million Latin American emigrants now reside in the US, making them the country's top ethnic minority. Yet alongside the US, other new destinations have appeared, with a substantial rise in flows towards Europe. Spain, in fact, has become the second-largest destination for emigrants outside of Latin America (Martínez Pizarro & Orrego Rivera, 2016).

Migration within the region, i.e. within Latin American countries, has persisted over time due to both geographic proximity and cultural affinities. This type of migration is quite frequent and has recently been particularly intense. According to data from the 2000 and 2010 censuses, migration between nations in the region was high during these years, with a rise of approximately 32 per cent in the number of Latin Americans living outside their home countries (Martínez Pizarro & Orrego Rivera, 2016). This trend has been attributed to the greater restrictions and higher costs of migrating to other continents, and also to the greater appeal of several countries in the region thanks to the economic expansion that was registered during this period.

Women have been the predominant Latin America emigrants since the 1980s, a trend that continues today and that strongly contrasts with migration norms in the past. One of its main drivers is the growing demand of care services in developed countries. This tendency is particularly strong in certain countries, such as Paraguay, where eighty men emigrate for every one hundred women, and the Dominican Republic, where fifty-five men emigrate for every one hundred women.

According to 2010 data, the main sending countries to other Latin American nations are Colombia, which had more than 900 000 people living in other countries within the region, and Paraguay, with nearly 600 000. Other countries with significant populations abroad include Bolivia (over 390 000) and Haiti and Nicaragua (nearly 300 000 each) (Martínez Pizarro & Orrego Rivera, 2016). In terms of the destinations chosen by these Latin American emigrants, Argentina, Costa Rica and Venezuela have historically been the region's migratory hubs. While the first two countries continue to attract foreign emigrants, Venezuela has lost its appeal and has also seen a very significant increase in its own emigrant population, a trend that became more acute in the second decade of the century in the context of the political and economic crisis that the country is currently experiencing.

After the turn of the century, the migration policies of a significant number of nations in the region have been amended to reflect international human rights accords. Several countries have made efforts to reduce obstacles to migration to protect people's right to migrate and live in another country. Other measures have also been implemented to increase the rights of migrants, fostering their social, political and economic integration. However, the lack of protections and affronts to the rights of many migrants in the region continues. One clear example is that of undocumented migrants in transit, especially those from Central America who enter Mexico with the goal of reaching the US. The bodily integrity of these migrants has been seriously compromised in recent years as a result of muggings, kidnappings and sexual and human trafficking, all part of a wave of violence and the rise of criminal groups in Mexico.

2.7 Summary

Latin America's current demographic profile reflects many long-term processes that exceed the specific economic and political context experienced throughout the region after the turn of the millennium. First, during the twentieth century, mass migrations from the countryside to cities led to intensive urbanisation. As a result, Latin America shifted from having a predominantly rural population to one of the most urbanised populations in the world today. Rural–urban migration has declined towards the end of the twentieth century, while flows between urban centres have become more prevalent. Second, since the mid twentieth century, Latin America has been a region characterised by emigration: the number of citizens living outside their countries of origin has been greater than the quantity of immigrants any country receives. Third, also since the mid twentieth century, Latin America has experienced profound changes in birth and mortality rates. These have resulted in longer life expectancies and a significant reduction in the number of children for women, which has led to an increase in the well-being of the population. Finally, since the last decades of the twentieth century, families began to undergo significant transformations in their structure and dynamics, leading to greater diversity in the forms of family living arrangements. But all these changes differ strongly among social class, ethnic groups and countries, and long-lasting problems of inequality persist.

These trends have created opportunities for the region and also posed challenges. In particular, we have noted the demographic window of opportunity that currently exists in Latin America, along with the inexorable process of population ageing, with consequences the region must address in coming decades. We have also highlighted the demands for care made increasingly acute and visible by the growing elderly population and the questioning of traditional gender roles, along with greater labour market participation among women. These issues have received increasing public attention but are still largely absent from government agendas and policies.

3 Inequality

This section describes income inequalities trends in Latin America, one of the world's most unequal regions. Despite the persistence of these inequalities over time, notable progress was made in the first years of the twenty-first century. The improvement was the result of several factors. On the one hand, a favourable international context and economic growth dynamised labour markets. On the other hand, the shift in the region's political trends translated into greater regulation of the labour market and redistributive policies, especially social transfers to the lowest-income households. Despite this remarkable progress, however, the recent drop in income inequality seems to have done little to alter the structural underpinnings of Latin American inequality. The concentration of property and wealth remains high; the redistributive effect on state policies has been limited; and there continue to be major gaps in the work conditions and salaries on the labour market.

3.1 The Drop in Inequality

During the first years of the twenty-first century, Latin America experienced several positive economic and social trends. Latin American economies grew enormously, due in part to a favourable international context – the commodity price boom, which upped the value of Latin American exports – and also due to the implementation of macroeconomic policies that helped increase national production in several countries. This growth was prolonged, from 2002 to 2014, with only a single pause (in 2009, the result of the global financial crisis). It was also intense, especially between 2002 and 2008, when the GDP per capita rose by 3.2 per cent annually on average (ECLAC, 2018). On the other hand, in sharp contrast to what had occurred in the last decades of the twentieth century, diverse social indicators also experienced favourable trends during these same years. According to ECLAC data, between 2002 and 2014, unemployment fell from 11.4 to 6.9 per cent; the quality of jobs improved; and there was a rise in real wages but, most importantly, in minimum wages. Poverty dropped significantly, from 43.9 to 28.2 per cent, in those same years, while the percentage of the population living in extreme poverty fell from 19.3 to 11.8 per cent (Figure 6).

In this context, income inequality also declined. As shown in a great number of studies, while the 1980s and 1990s were marked by ever-increasing income concentration in Latin America, the trend reversed itself at the dawn of the new century (Alvaredo & Gasparini, 2015; Cornia, 2014; ECLAC, 2018; Hoffman

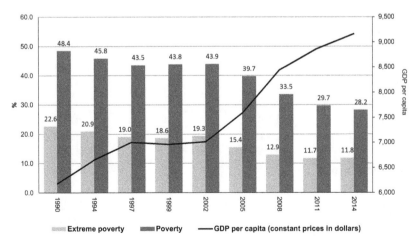

Figure 6 Latin America and the Caribbean: GDP per capita, poverty and extreme poverty, 1990–2014.

Source: ECLAC, based on data from Household Surveys Database (BADEHOG)

& Centeno, 2003; Lustig, López-Calva & Ortiz-Juarez, 2011). According to the ECLAC average for Latin America countries, the Gini index, which ranges from 0 (complete equality) to 1 (complete inequality), dropped from 0.547 in 2002 to 0.491 in 2014 (Table 1). During these years, the gap between the highest and lowest income earners also shrunk: while the 20 per cent richest households earned on average 22 times what the 20 per cent poorest households were earning in 2002, that gap had fallen to 16 times in 2014.

The reduction of inequality is noteworthy not only because it diverges with the trends of previous decades but also because it happened in nearly every country. In this regard, the tendency was regional, though its intensity varied from country to country. In general terms, inequality reduction was greater in the Andean and Southern Cone nations and less in Central America and Mexico. The countries that made the most progress in reducing inequality

Table 1 Latin America: Gini index of income inequality, circa 1990, 2002 and 2014

	1990	2002	2014
Argentina[a]	0.501	0.578	0.470
Bolivia (PS)	0.537	0.614	0.491
Brazil	0.627	0.634	0.548
Chile	0.554	0.552	0.509
Colombia	0.601	0.567	0.535
Costa Rica	0.438	0.488	0.505
Ecuador[a]	0.461	0.513	0.447
El Salvador	0.507	0.525	0.436
Guatemala	0.582	0.542	0.553
Honduras	0.615	0.588	0.564
Mexico	0.536	0.514	0.491
Nicaragua	0.582	0.579	0.478
Panama	0.530	0.567	0.519
Paraguay	0.447	0.558	0.536
Peru	–	0.525	0.439
Dominican Republic	–	0.537	0.519
Uruguay[a]	0.416	0.455	0.379
Venezuela (BR)	0.471	0.500	0.407
Latin America[b]	0.509	0.547	0.491

[a] Urban areas.

[b] Simple average: circa 1990, urban areas, sixteen countries; circa 2002 and 2014, eighteen countries.

Source: ECLAC, based on data from Household Surveys Database (BADEHOG)

were Bolivia, Venezuela, Argentina and Uruguay, with drops in the Gini index of more than 4 per cent annually between 2002 and 2014 (Amarante & Colacce, 2018).

However, income distribution did not continue to improve over time. The most progress occurred during the first years of the century, and the reductions later stalled or even halted. The trajectories reflected economic dynamics and most social indicators. In fact, although Latin American economies continued to grow after 2008, they did so at a slower rate. The GDP per inhabitant in the region grew at an annual rate of 1.7 per cent between 2008 and 2012; between 2012 and 2014, it grew by 0.8 per cent; and in 2015, it experienced negative growth (ECLAC, 2018). In this process, the new international context undoubtedly played a role, due to the fall in the prices of export products. Labour markets lost their impetus; there was a gradual drop in the improvements to job quality, and by 2015, unemployment had risen. Poverty would also be impacted by these changes. The number of people living in poverty and extreme poverty, both of which had dropped slightly between 2012 and 2014, rose in 2015. In the case of inequality, the trends are highly similar. The reduction of the regional Gini index was 1.5 per cent annually on average between 2002 and 2008; 0.7 per cent between 2008 and 2014; and just 0.4 per cent between 2014 and 2016 (ECLAC, 2018).

The fact that the downward trend in the region's inequality has slowed to a halt is concerning because, despite the improvements, inequality continues to be very high in Latin America. One of the world's most unequal regions, Latin America is second only to sub-Saharan Africa (Alvaredo & Gasparini, 2015). When the analysis goes beyond the regional average, however, there are important differences in the levels of inequality across Latin America. In 2014, for example, the Gini index for countries like Brazil, Colombia, Guatemala, Honduras and Paraguay was higher than 0.53, while in Uruguay, the least unequal of the region's countries, the Gini was under 0.40 (Table 1). However, in comparison with other regions in the world, the variation between countries is lower in Latin America. The inequality gap between countries in the region is less pronounced than in other regions, but this is because of the relatively high level of inequality in nearly all countries (Alvaredo & Gasparini, 2015). High inequality is, in this regard, a structural feature shared by almost all Latin American countries. The region is more unequal than what could be expected given its income level, which suggests it could be suffering from 'excessive inequality' (Londoño & Székely, 2000). This means that the living standards of a large portion of the population are worse than what would be expected in view of the region's economic development.

3.2 The Economic and Political Context

In Latin America the persistent income inequality is related to long data inequalities of class, gender and ethnicity (Hoffman & Centeno, 2003). Historically, variations in inequality have depended primarily on macroeconomic policy, economic performance, labour market dynamics, state regulations of all markets (goods and services, labour, financial etc.), tax systems, public spending and demographic trends. What explains the reduction in income inequality during the first years of the twenty-first century in Latin America? An extensive literature has already addressed this question. As noted in Bértola and Williamson (2017), one conclusion stemming from the research is that the fall in income inequality cannot be attributed to a single cause. On the one hand, demographic trends play a role, even if they were not the main driving factor. The increase of remittances, the decrease in the relative size of households, drops in fertility in the poorer segments of society and female labour force participation rates had an impact on the drop in inequality (Gasparini, Cruces & Tornarolli, 2016).

On the other hand, there are no doubts about the key role played by the favourable global economy and its impact on regional economic growth. But this factor alone is seemingly not enough to account for the drop in inequality. Certain countries saw inequality decline even without the impact of the commodity price boom, and there are similar moments in the history of Latin America in which inequality rose instead of falling. In this regard, other factors also contributed to this reduction, though to varying degrees in each country. One particularly relevant trend that occurred during the first years of the new century was the 'pink tide' in politics across the region.

Filgueira et al. (2012) mentions that this shift to the left can be seen as the result of the incorporation crisis that characterised the final decades of the twentieth century, when neo-liberal policies and structural adjustment programmes were the norm. This incorporation crisis responded to a growing gap between diverging social processes. On the one hand, heightened aspirations for consumption and social mobility became increasingly viewed as legitimate demands, the result of expanded electoral democracies, urbanisation, rising education indexes and the exposure to new consumer patterns through new and widely available technologies. On the other hand, the mechanisms that would allow these new and growing aspirations to be satisfied were not in place, due to limited job opportunities, growing poverty and inequality and the lack of opportunities for social mobility.

In this context, social issues in the region began to rise on political agendas. One of the most visible manifestations of this 'politicisation' of social problems

(Roberts, 2012) was the election of left and centre-left administrations. While campaigning, these candidates had promised social inclusion and vowed to reverse the deteriorated living standards that a great portion of the population had suffered during the years of neo-liberalism. Between 1998 and 2011, eleven countries in the region elected presidents from the left or centre left, leading to a situation without precedent in the region's history: two-thirds of Latin Americans were living under left-leaning national administrations (Levitsky & Roberts, 2011). Though there were notable differences among them, these administrations shared – though to varying degrees – redistributive public policies.

However, the drop on inequality was not limited to countries with left-leaning administrations but applied to almost all Latin American countries, even those whose administrations had different political orientations. This was the case of Colombia, Peru, El Salvador and Panama. In any case, it appears clear that during this stage, a new post-neo-liberal political agenda was imposed, albeit to varying degrees, in the countries of Latin America, and social issues topped this agenda. The triumph of left-leaning parties and movements in some countries was a sign of this new agenda, though it also contributed to shaping it. In this context, as noted by Roberts (2012), the institutionalisation of democratic competition in the region appears to have led governments with divergent ideologies to offer some type of response to the renewed demands for social inclusion. Redistributive policies were thus not exclusive to left or centre-left parties; they were also present to a certain degree in governments across the political spectrum and mainly took shape as social policies focused on the most vulnerable populations.

3.3 The Key Variables: Labour Income and Social Transfers

What were the specific factors that contributed – in different combinations, and to varying degrees, depending on the country – to reducing inequality in Latin America? One of the main findings of the studies on inequality is that a great part of the decline can be attributed to decreased labour income dispersion. The second most important factor is improved non-labour income distribution, mainly due to social transfers for the poorest households, including conditional cash transfers and non-contributory pensions for the elderly (de la Torre, Messina & Silva, 2017; Levy & Schady, 2013).

The key factor for understanding improved dispersion of labour income was the drop on skill premiums, which led to a reduction in the income gaps between workers with varying skill levels. To explain this change, generally arguments focus on mechanisms of supply and demand. The expansion of education access in the region in recent decades has modified the composition of the workforce, substantially increasing the supply of skilled workers (Lustig, López-Calva & Ortiz-Juarez, 2011). Thus, for example, the percentage of workers with only an elementary school education in 1990 was 47.2 per cent in Argentina, 49.3 per cent in Chile and 77 per cent in Brazil. By 2013, these percentages had diminished significantly, dropping to a minimum of 17.7 per cent in Argentina and a maximum of 34.3 per cent in Brazil. On the other hand, the percentage of workers who had finished high school and accessed higher education also increased (Fernández & Messina, 2017). This higher supply of skilled workers could already be seen in the 1990s. Since the turn of the new century, however, this coincided with a greater creation of jobs and with a shift in labour demand, which targeted the least skilled workers (de la Torre, Messina & Silva, 2017; Gasparini, Cruces & Tornarolli, 2011).

But the improved wage dispersion also corresponded to labour market institutions taking a more active role. The renewed collective bargaining power that unions obtained in more favourable economic and political contexts and the labour regulation policies introduced by states to improve working conditions and wages both contributed enormously to reducing the inequality between skilled and unskilled workers, particularly in certain countries in South America. Maurizio (2014), for example, has shown how the increase in the minimum wage, received by the least qualified workers – those at the lower end of wage dispersion – explains a significant part in the drop in income inequality in Argentina, Brazil and Uruguay. Similarly, Amarante and Arim (2015) have shown how in Brazil, Ecuador and Uruguay, the expansion of labour regulations and the reduction of informality contributed to reducing inequality.

Although the improvement to labour income distribution was the most important factor in reducing inequality in the region as a whole, social transfers to low-income households also play a role.

In this period, social transfers have become a permanent policy, not simply one implemented to help the poor weather a crisis, as was common in the past. Its introduction in a great many Latin American countries can be seen as a sign of the change in the region's political agenda, as mentioned above. During the first decade of the new century, there was some consensus on poverty as a grave social issue requiring active state policies. Conditional cash transfers and non-contributory pensions, two state mechanisms targeting the lowest-income households, were the main ways the state addressed this demand. This policy has been introduced by administrations with different political and ideological profiles, even among those that lean towards orthodox economic policies and have no intention of continuing to improve inequality with redistributive measures of other sorts.

Conditional cash transfer programmes typically provide an income for poor families with children; in exchange for the cash, families must take certain measures to develop their children's human capital, like ensuring children get check-ups and attend school regularly. These programmes began to be implemented at the end of the 1990s and quickly expanded throughout the region. In 2013, 135 million people from seventeen countries, or 25 per cent of Latin America's population, were enrolled in a programme of this kind (Table 2). In certain countries with a history of weak social policies, the percentage of the populations enrolled in transfer programmes is even higher. The case of Bolivia is particularly noteworthy, as more than half the population is covered by programmes of this sort. Even in countries like Paraguay, El Salvador and Honduras, which tended to allocate very little to social assistance programmes and where coverage is especially limited, a high portion of the population receives conditional cash transfers.

These programmes have proven very cost-effective. By providing the lowest-income groups with an income, cash transfers have helped improve living conditions and lessen poverty in beneficiary households. They have also helped increase school attendance and reduce child labour. Furthermore, they have achieved all of this without a hefty investment: the percentage of the national budget allocated to these programmes is very low, representing on average 0.34 per cent of the GDP in 2013 (Table 2). Cash transfers have also contributed to reducing inequality, although evidence suggests a high degree of cross-country variation. In general terms, cash transfers have had some effect mainly due to the fact that they are well targeted in lower-income groups. In contrast, the small amounts of the programmes have put limits on their distributive impact (Amarante & Brun, 2018; Soares et al., 2009).

At the same time, numerous countries have reformed their social security systems in order to expand the coverage of non-contributory pension schemes. These schemes generally target elderly adults deprived of the right to ordinary pensions, that is, the pensions resulting from a worker's contributions to social security over the course of his or her time working. In Latin America, labour market trajectories marked by unstable and informal employment have resulted in a great number of elderly people who do not qualify for regular pensions.

By 2013, more than 33 per cent of elderly adults in the region were receiving non-contributory pensions. Nevertheless, the differences between countries were significant. While some countries, such as Bolivia, implemented universal pensions, most – like Mexico and Brazil – restricted them to individuals not receiving any contributory pensions. Finally, in some cases like that of Peru and Colombia, mechanisms were designed to ensure such pensions reached poor senior citizens (Robles, Rubio & Stampini, 2015). In Argentina, the social

Table 2 Conditional cash transfer programmes in Latin America and the Caribbean, 2013

| Country | Programme | Coverage | | Budget (% of GDP) |
		Population (× 1000)	Population (%)	
Argentina	Asignación Universal por Hijo	8383	20.2	0.47
Bolivia (PS)	Bono Juancito Pinto	5786	52.4	0.19
Brazil	Bolsa Família	57 753	28.7	0.44
Chile	Chile Solidario (Ingreso Ético Familiar)	754	4.3	0.13
Colombia	Familias en Acción	11 263	23.9	0.23
Costa Rica	Avancemos	641	13.6	0.17
Dominican Republic	Progresando con Solidaridad	2324	22.3	0.46
Ecuador	Bono de Desarrollo Humano	4290	27.2	0.66
El Salvador	Comunidades Solidarias Rurales y Urbanas	620	9.8	0.06
Guatemala	Mi Família Progresa	3810	24.6	0.20
Honduras	Bono 10 Mil	1228	15.2	0.86
Jamaica	Programme of Advancement Through Health and Education	540	19.4	0.27
Mexico	Oportunidades	32 340	27.3	0.22
Panama	Red de Oportunidades	353	9.5	0.12
Paraguay	Tekoporã	395	5.8	0.09
Peru	Juntos	3819	12.3	0.14
Uruguay	Asignaciones Familiares (Plan Equidad)	791	23.3	0.40
LAC[a]		135 001	24.8	0.34

[a] Population-weighted average.

Source: Robles, Rubio and Stampini (2015, Table A2)

security policy stood out because it involved not only non-contributory pensions but contributory ones as well. There was a significant increase in access to the contributory pension system thanks to efforts to integrate people who had worked in the informal sector as well as housewives. This policy was important to limit inequality in the access to social security rights among beneficiaries of contributory and non-contributory pensions, given that the amounts of the non-contributory pensions are significantly lower. In most countries of Latin America, however, contributory systems suffered no modifications whatsoever, and thus coverage continues to be limited.

Owing to the importance that social transfers acquired during this period, some researchers have criticised the so-called post-neo-liberal administrations for investing more in individual consumption than in transportation, health care, education and other public goods or service.

However, increased consumer finance for the poor should be interpreted from the perspective of what occurred during the previous period. The 1980s and 1990s were years of economic hardship with a severe impact on the well-being of many Latin Americans. People's ability to pay for the basic upkeep of a home, purchase goods like clothing or home appliances and pay for services like health care or recreation was significantly diminished. As a result, at the turn of the new century, there was a consumption deficit among a great part of the population. It would be appropriate to speak of a 'debt to consumers' in the region, and the post-neo-liberal governments in Latin America made efforts precisely to reduce this debt.

The other important goal of post-neo-liberal governments was to support industrialisation, and the increase in consumer finance for the poor was a key tool to achieving this. To borrow from the arguments of Latin America structuralism, the weakness of domestic markets represented a serious obstacle to local industrialisation. Therefore, the government objective of fostering consumption was also associated with a strategy based on long-term economic ideas.

On the other hand, despite allegations to the contrary, these administrations also made investments in public goods. According to data, countries in the region increased their social expenditures. In fact, the social expenditures of the public sector reached historic highs in the region, 14.5 per cent of the GDP, in 2015 (ECLAC, 2017). As household consumption rose, there was also investment in housing, health care, education and basic infrastructure. It is possible, however, that some countries were not able to strike a successful balance between their investment in public goods versus private goods. Undoubtedly, Latin America suffers from a high 'infrastructure gap' (Rozas, 2010), that is, the gap between what the region possesses in terms of infrastructure and what it would require to accompany growth, due both to historical shortcomings and to the economic growth in the past decade.

But the context that allowed for the reduction of inequality during the first decade of the twenty-first century has changed. This is owed, as we have noted, to shifts in the world order and a deceleration of economic growth since 2010. This has slowed the impetus of labour markets in the region and decreased their potential to continue to cut down inequality. On the other hand, the political context also changed. Since the mid 2010s, there has been a shift in politics across the region. In many countries, this meant an end to the left and centre-left administrations that had been ruling until then. In this new context, the question of whether redistributive policies will be expanded – or even whether they will continue – is now in doubt. And though conditional cash transfers have remained strong on the whole, it does not appear likely that they will have a further impact on inequality. As noted by Amarante and Colacce (2018), the broad level of coverage of such transfers limits the distributive effect of future expansions. At the same time, the conditions do not appear to be in place for increasing the amounts paid, due to the new political context and the fiscal constraints that the region is currently facing.

3.4 The Persistence of a Regressive Tax Structure

What does appear clear is that the redistributive role of the state continues to be limited in Latin America. This is due to the fact that, as mentioned earlier, there could have been more efforts to improve the living conditions of the poorest sectors – as seen in the low budgets for conditional cash transfers – but also and fundamentally because tax systems continue to have a very low impact on redistribution. It is true that during this period, some advances were made in this regard. On the one hand, the tax burden increased significantly, rising nearly 60 per cent on average between 1990 and 2014, from 13.2 to 21.0 per cent of the GDP. On the other hand, many countries introduced reforms to their tax systems in order to increase the share of progressive income tax within total tax revenue. In particular, countries did increase such revenues with different systems of extraction, royalties and commercial agreements regarding natural resources, especially mineral, such as in Ecuador and Bolivia (Gómez Sabaini, Jiménez & Morán, 2017). However, tax collection in the region is still far from the tax revenue to GDP ratio of developed countries (over 30 per cent of GDP). In addition, the portion of tax revenues collected from indirect taxes (sales tax) continues to be particularly high, which generally determines the regressive nature of the system as a whole (Gómez Sabaiani & Morán, 2017).

The low levels of personal income tax in Latin America can be attributed to a series of factors, including low maximum rates, limits on taxable incomes (due to a great number of exemptions and deductions) and the high levels of evasion and arrears. One important limitation on this tax in the region is that it is mainly collected from wage workers, that is, formal sector workers whose taxes are withheld from their salaries. This affects tax equality, since wage workers bear the greatest burden, while independent workers are more likely not only to evade taxes but also to benefit from preferential treatment in the capital gains taxes, either because they are in a lower tax bracket or because they are exempt from such taxes (Jiménez, 2017).

A comparison of Latin America's fiscal policy with that of other countries reveals that it has only a meagre redistributive effect. In the OECD countries, the inequality of market income before state intervention is only slightly inferior to that observed in the countries of Latin America. When fiscal policy is considered, there are notable differences: in OECD countries, the Gini index drops 35 per cent after government transfers and taxes, while in LATAM, it falls just 6 per cent (Figure 7). Thus, despite the improvements to the state's redistributive capacity in recent years, major reforms – especially tax reforms – still appear to be necessary.

3.5 Light and Shadows in the Labour Market

The reduction of inequality through the labour market has also faced structural limitations. Indeed, economic growth, along with the implementation of more active labour policy design in some countries, has led to significant improvement in various indicators. However, the productive structures of Latin American countries underwent few changes, which limited the possibility of decreasing inequality through the creation of better-quality and higher-paying jobs.

There were numerous positive trends in labour, in contrast to the deterioration suffered by labour markets during the previous period. First, there was an acceleration of job creation, which led to growth in the employment rate. This was particularly intense until the 2009 crisis. During this period, Latin American economies showed a greater capacity for job creation than they did during the 1990s; for example, while between 1991 and 2002, an economic growth of 3 per cent was accompanied by a slight recession in the urban employment rate, between 2003 and 2012, the same rate of growth led to a 0.4 point increase in the employment rate (Weller, 2017).

The growth in job creation brought about a fall in the unemployment rate, such that the average in the region dropped from 11.4 per cent to 6.9 per cent in 2014, ending the trend of growth this indicator showed during the 1990s. At the same time, working conditions and remuneration improved substantially. There was also progress with regard to work protection, as shown by the percentage of workers covered by a pension system, which increased from 38.3 per cent in 2002 to 50.3 per cent in 2015 (ECLAC, 2018). This greater protection was the

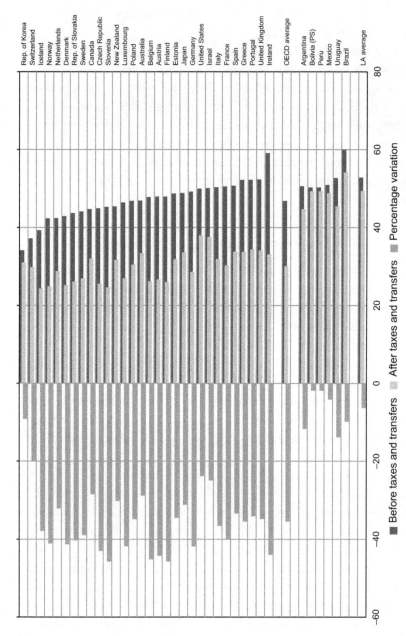

Figure 7 Gini index before and after taxes and transfers.

Source: ECLAC (2014b)

result of a combination of factors. A significant portion of new jobs created during the period was registered wage employment, but at the same time, workers who had not been previously covered were incorporated into protection systems. These processes were underpinned by active state policies: voluntary affiliation of independent workers and a strengthening of labour inspection and labour registration incentives for historically unprotected groups (such as micro-business employees, rural workers or domestic service workers), among others (Salazar-Xirinachs & Chacaltana, 2018).

Meanwhile, there was a decrease in low-productivity employment in the informal sector (measured as the percentage of workers in micro-businesses, low-qualification independent workers and domestic service workers). Informality is a persistent and structural feature in Latin America, associated with the limitations historically shown by the productive structures of countries in the region to create jobs for the entire population (see Centeno & Portes, 2006). People working in the informal sector are in worse conditions than other workers. They more frequently experience unstable employability and no access to social benefits. Their incomes tend to be irregular, in many cases below the poverty line or barely above it, and during periods of economic crisis, they have a higher probability of losing their jobs. For all these reasons, the reduction shown in the percentage of informal workers during this period, of nearly 5 points between 2002 and 2013 (from 54.0 per cent to 49.3 per cent), was a particularly relevant trend (ECLAC, 2016).

This favourable economic situation and employment performance fomented an increase in workers' incomes. According to data from ECLAC (2018), on average in Latin America between 2005 and 2015, monthly real wages increased by 19.8 per cent, though there were significant differences between countries. The largest increases took place in the Southern Cone, while countries in the Andean region were close to the regional average, and Central American countries and Mexico were far below it. The improvement in work income was supported in some countries by a more active role for unions, the reactivation of collective bargaining and the implementation of diverse governmental wage policies. With regard to the latter, efforts to support minimum wages were particularly relevant and led to a recorded average real increase of 42 per cent between 2005 and 2015.

All of these improvements were noteworthy but had clear limitations: first, because the positive evolution of work indicators was not sustained over time; second, because some indicators still show troubling values. Nearly half of workers do not have access to work protection systems, and a similar proportion work in the informal sector in low-productivity activities. The rate of employees earning wages below the minimums established in each country is still very high, nearly 40 per cent, and employment does not guarantee the satisfaction of basic needs, such that the income of many employees is below the poverty line. Finally, although there was a reduction in inequality between different social groups in several areas, there are still significant gaps. For example, ECLAC (2018) shows that labour protection is 2.5 times higher among urban employees than among their rural counterparts (55 per cent vs. 22 per cent in 2015) and 4 times higher in the formal sector than in the informal (69 per cent vs. 17 per cent). Likewise, although the gender wage gap decreased during the period, men continue to earn 1.3 times more than women ($856 vs. $636 in monthly purchasing power parity in 2015). And while average income in urban areas is 2.2 times higher than that in rural areas ($804 vs. $363), the high-productivity formal sector enjoys an income 2.3 times higher than that of the informal sector ($1051 vs. $457).

Overall, because Latin American countries did not show significant change in production, improvements in the labour market did not exceed the increase driven by an expansive economic cycle and a favourable political context regarding labour protection. Latin American economies are still characterised by insufficient development and production diversification, so there have been no structural changes in the area of labour. In general terms, labour markets in the region are still plagued by an insufficient offering of employment in the medium- and high-productivity sectors, significant gaps in work quality and wages that, to a high degree, are below those required in order to overcome poverty and achieve adequate levels of well-being.

3.6 Distributive Improvements and the Middle Classes

The distributive improvements that the region experienced during the period involved substantial mobility and modifications in the weight and characteristics of certain social groups. One of the biggest transformations in this regard has been the expansion of the so-called new middle classes. Historically considered a minority in the region – except in some countries – the middle classes appear to have grown during the first part of the twenty-first century. During this period, as Latin American societies became more egalitarian, new middle classes have emerged, as noted in many different areas. In societies seen as polarised, the growth of these new middle classes appeared to contribute to social cohesion and political stability.

The new middle classes are indicative of the population's enhanced purchasing power. The many studies that analyse the growth of these middle classes tend to classify them empirically based on income level (among others, Birdsall, 2007; Castellani, Parent & Zenteno, 2014; López-Calva & Ortiz-Juarez, 2014;

Lora & Fajardo, 2013). These studies reveal the conspicuous expansion of middle-income groups since the turn of the new century, an expansion that can be attributed to the rise in salaries that accompanied economic growth and diverse policies that increased the lowest-income group threshold.

Some authors emphasise that a true 'democratisation of consumption' took hold as part of this process, allowing a growing number of population groups to attain goods and services previously out of their reach. It is thus also plausible that in certain countries of the region historically characterised by less inequality – like Argentina or Uruguay – the process has taken on a different meaning: the recovery of sectors that saw a decrease in their purchasing power during the 1980s and 1990s. In both cases, the growing presence of mass consumer goods in all the underprivileged neighbourhoods of Latin America represented a strong contrast with previous decades of deprivation. Goods like computers and cell phones, previously unattainable for the poor, have become easier to purchase in recent years. This increased purchasing power was underpinned, in turn, by greater 'financialisation' among the lowest income sectors and by a long-term trend of price drops for durable goods.

From classic sociological perspectives in which social classes are divided based on their status in employment, the new middle classes comprise a heterogeneous group that mainly includes working classes whose living standards have improved. In other words, this isn't about the emergence of a new class, as that would imply more structural and occupation-based upward social mobility processes. From this perspective, the great change in the period is the process of social inclusion and improved standards of living that the most underprivileged groups of society can access.

In any case, the debate on the new middle classes, their identity and their social behaviour has been widely addressed in academia and in the media. Some of the findings highlight the heterogeneity of these groups. In Brazil, for example, research has shown that the new middle classes can be conservative or progressive, on the political left or right, cosmopolitan or nationalistic (Tavares de Almeida, 2017). In contrast, the images of the new middle classes in Peru are more homogeneous: they are described as more nationalistic and conservative, less progressive and more ethnically mixed than previous Peruvian middle classes (Arellano Cueva, 2010).

While the first works on the new middle classes emphasised the multiple economic, social and political benefits that their growth could bring, more recent investigations have emphasised their financial fragility and political dissatisfaction. On the one hand, though their situation is not characterised by poverty, it is characterised by vulnerability (Birdsall, Lustig & Meyer, 2014; Castellani, Parent & Zenteno, 2014). A portion of this new middle class has a highly unstable status in employment, especially because of the high prevalence of informal occupations. This means that a change in the economic context could lead to a loss of the improved living standards. On the other hand, middle classes across the region appear to share one common feature: dissatisfaction. They feel insecure due to their financial fragility and fearful of losing their recently acquired well-being. They criticise their governments for high crime rates and for the poor health care and education systems. They argue that they pay more and more taxes taxes but do not use public services: as soon as they are able, they send their children to private schools, get private health insurance and live in gated neighbourhoods. Paradoxically, the new middle classes are one of the most successful offshoots of the post-neo-liberal administrations but also one of their most vociferous critics.

The redistribution process not only led to the emergence of the new middle classes but also appears to have altered the relative position of the traditional middle classes. In fact, although these groups seem to have increased their purchasing power in absolute terms as the economy has expanded, it is possible that at the same time, their relative position has eroded. This is not only because the expansion of the new middle classes meant that groups less privileged than themselves have approached them socially but also because they appear to have lost their relative positions. This occurred, in part, because of the labour market dynamics. It is likely that the reduction of the income gap between skilled and unskilled workers hit the upper middle classes particularly hard, due to their high levels of education. On the other hand, because they work and mainly interact with the formal economy, it is likely that the most privileged groups were affected by the increased tax burden during this period, given the weight of sales and wage taxes in the region's tax systems.

3.7 The Concentration of Income and Wealth

Inequality is mainly owed to the high concentration of income and wealth among society's most privileged members. It is thus impossible to comprehend the true dimension of recent trends without including the upper classes in our analysis. Reconstructing what occurred with this social sector, however, is no easy task. Unlike the middle and lower classes, the upper classes are largely invisible from a statistical point of view. Information on their incomes and wealth is scarce and highly fragmented. Research on inequality in Latin America and worldwide is typically based on household surveys, the main source of data on available income in most countries. Yet these surveys have serious limitations when it comes to reporting the income of the rich. This is not only because the wealthy are reluctant to respond to such questions but also because of sampling limitations. High incomes are significantly underestimated, especially those non-labour, like profits. One very important consequence of this is that measures of income concentration like the Gini index only partially reflect the scope of inequality. Household surveys also do not provide information on assets, which is fundamental information for a description of the upper classes.

In recent times, social scientists have expressed growing interest in the high-income threshold, which has led to significant efforts to reconstruct this group's incomes and assets using other data sources. Although most of these studies have been conducted in developed countries, there are some on Latin America. The findings of these works reveal how our knowledge on the scope of inequality would be altered if more adequate data sources were considered and additionally raise doubts as to the true scope of current trends.

Once of the novel strategies increasingly used to incorporate the highest income groups to the analysis involves drawing data from tax returns (though these are not immune from severe underreporting, either). Studies conducted in Argentina, Colombia and Uruguay show how, when this alternative information source is used, the concentration of income is much more top heavy than suggested by household surveys though, in general terms, still reflects the decline in inequality during the first decade of the century (Alvaredo & Londoño, 2014; Alvaredo & Piketty, 2010; Burdín, Esponda & Vigorito, 2014).

On the other hand, data about the functional income distribution and the distribution of wealth reveal the limits of recent trends. The functional focus on distribution evaluates the labour share of the GDP based on the data from the national account systems. In other words, the focus is on the distribution of income not between isolated individuals but between capital and labour. Studies that have taken this approach show that in the 2000s, there was an increased participation of the wage share in the GDP, but it was not as widespread as that which results from an analysis of the evolution of the Gini index with household survey data (ECLAC, 2017).

A joint analysis of these trends provides a more realistic perspective with regard to what has happened in recent times. Although the drop in the Gini index is a fact, its impact is limited. The lion's share of the reduction in inequality is owed to a fairer distribution of income among workers, but the portion of total wealth corresponding to this group remains virtually unchanged. In most of the countries of Latin America, workers did not improve their status with regard to capital.

Oxfam (2015) shows that inequality is much more profound in Latin America if the focus turns to wealth and assets, beyond an analysis of income. In 2013–14, the 10 per cent richest in the region earned 37 per cent of the income, but the differences were even more extreme if, instead of income, wealth and assets were considered. In that case, the 10 per cent wealthiest accumulate 71 per cent of wealth and assets and the top 1 per cent 41 per cent of the total. Levels of inequality are particularly extreme in relation to landownership, in a region that tops the worldwide ranking in concentration. In Paraguay, for example, 80 per cent of farmlands are owned by 1.6 per cent of landowners, while in Guatemala, an estimated 80 per cent of lands belong to just 8 per cent of producers.

The figures in the World Ultra Wealth Report 2014 on multi-millionaires in Latin America (individuals with US$30 million or more in net worth) are quite telling. A few examples provide an idea of the magnitude of the concentration of wealth in the region. According to the report, there are an estimated 14.805 multi-millionaires in Latin America whose wealth is equivalent to 35 per cent of the regional GDP. This is a quantity of money similar to what would be needed to eliminate monetary poverty in Brazil, Colombia, El Salvador, Guatemala, Honduras, Mexico, Nicaragua and Peru. In Honduras, the fortune amassed by the country's multi-millionaires is 1.5 times the country's GDP. The wealth of Paraguay's multi-millionaires is 25 times the country's health care budget and 20 times its education budget, while in El Salvador and Guatemala, the riches of these tycoons stand at 19 times the health care budget and 27 times the education budget.

Over the course of the decade, there seems to have been no reduction in the concentration of wealth and property, and even some indication that it could have increased (Oxfam, 2015). According to *Forbes* magazine, for example, the riches of the region's billionaires rose 21 per cent annually between 2002 and 2015, an increase that is 6 times higher than the region's GDP growth (3.5 per cent annually). In other words, a great part of the economic growth from the period appears to have been captured by the wealthiest members of society.

3.8 Tolerance for Inequality

From the information presented in this section, it appears that the improvements in income distribution did little to change the structural underpinnings of inequality in Latin America. This is because, first and foremost, property and wealth continued to be as concentrated as they ever were, if not more so. Second, because despite some progress, tax policy continued to have only a limited redistributive effect, particularly due to the little taxes paid by the highest income groups. Finally, this is because unskilled jobs continue to represent the lion's share of jobs available on labour markets, with salaries that often do not allow workers to emerge from poverty.

These facts lead us to a fundamental aspect of income inequality in the region today: the specifics of the new post-neo-liberal political agenda and the limits to the support for recent left and centre-left administrations. During the first years of the new century, several indicators suggested diminished social tolerance for inequality. According to surveys, a greater percentage of Latin Americans believed that inequality was an issue their society should address (Blofield & Luna, 2011). Inequality also became an important topic among scholars, political parties, social movements and international organisations. However, reducing inequality is an arduous task, especially if the aim is 'equality of places' (Dubet, 2012), that is, shorter distances between social classes. In this regard, the new post-neo-liberal political agenda, which focused attention once again on Latin America's historic social deficits, appears to have been based on a consensus more centred on social inclusion than on equality.

In fact, for years, these left and centre-left administrations enjoyed the support of broad social coalitions comprising different groups that had suffered the effects of the neo-liberal administrations. Marginal sectors, industrial workers and impoverished middle classes provided the initial social support for the post-neo-liberal governments, but so did human rights organisations and feminist, indigenous and Afro-Latino associations. This support laid the foundation for policies aimed at reducing the most extreme forms of exclusion, an offshoot of policies from the 1990s and others dating back even further. In other words, when the objective was to reduce the most extreme expressions of social exclusion, social coalitions provided broad support.

But it should not be assumed that the social coalitions that stood behind policies for social inclusion were also willing to lend their support to a reduction of inequality. Why? Because, the search for equality is quite demanding. All public policies, as well as a good deal of private actions, have an impact on equality and inequality. Investment in infrastructure, a plan for citizen security, a model for developing industry: all favour certain social groups, certain regions, certain age groups, and not others. For that reason, the push for quality should serve as a lens for analysing each and every policy. In addition, equality not only demands increased living standards for the lowest-income population – through social transfers, non-contributory pensions and even minimum wage; it also necessitates measures that reduce the extreme concentration of income and assets. In other words, equality cries out for a focus on the lower classes, but a focus on the middle and upper classes as well. It even calls for redistribution among workers: unionised workers in a more favourable position need to agree to discuss an eventual redistribution of a portion of their benefits to less protected workers and those in the informal sector. In any case, the significant reduction of inequality in recent years means that on the whole, groups in the most favourable positions were willing to surrender resources and privileges. This dimension of inequality was rarely incorporated into the post-neo-liberal political agendas, and when it was, it met with strong social opposition.

3.9 Summary

The reduction in inequality that Latin America experienced during the first years of the twenty-first century is noteworthy because of its scope, but also because it contrasted with what had occurred in the last decades of the twentieth century when top-heavy income concentration consolidated Latin America's position as one of the most unequal regions in the world. The improvement was the result of several factors. On the one hand, a favourable international context and economic growth dynamised labour markets, especially the demand for unskilled labour, in a context marked by a greater supply of highly educated workers. On the other hand, the shift in the region's political trends translated into greater regulation of the labour market and redistributive policies, especially social transfers to the lowest-income households.

Despite this remarkable progress, however, the recent drop in income inequality seems to have done little to alter the structural underpinnings of Latin American inequality. The concentration of property and wealth remains high; the redistributive effect on state policies has been limited; and there continue to be major gaps in the work conditions and salaries on the labour market. This evidence brings up questions related to the specific contents of the new post-neo-liberal political agenda and to the degree of social consensus on the implementation of profound reforms in the area within most of the countries in the region.

Recent changes in the economic and political context have halted the improvements in income distribution. In this context, two questions must be addressed: to what extent these changes will produce a trend in the opposite direction (towards a new rise in inequality in the region) and, if that does occur, whether the population will tolerate a rise in inequality and the reversal of the progress made during these years.

4 Education, Health and Housing

This section is focused on education, health and housing. We analyse the main indicators related to standards of living and inequality, in particular educational coverage and quality; epidemiological profile and population state of health as well as conditions of housing. The feature shared by all three spheres is an improvement in absolute indicators, as has been observed with regard to income. Indeed, these improvements have occurred in many cases prior to the period studied, but they have also been stimulated by increased public investment and an improved economic situation in general. As a result, there is more coverage than in the past, but strong differences in accessibility and in the quality of services for different classes and groups, such as indigenous and Afro–Latin American, remain.

4.1 Extending Education Coverage: A Successful Process

Coverage and quality are the two main indicators in education. Coverage shows the relation between offer and demand in each education cycle. It's an indicator of educational access for different groups and ages. Quality is about the incorporation of cognitive abilities among students, differences in education from school to school and the imbalance between content and the needs of the production system. Latin America has been successful in the extension of coverage, but quality gaps remain a big problem.

In 1960, only half of children attended primary school; in 1980, that figure was 80 per cent, and it has risen to nearly universal levels at present (Tedesco, 2012). The secondary education rate in Latin America was 36.4 per cent in 1975, 49.7 per cent in 1985 and 62.2 per cent in 1997, growing more than worldwide averages (OREAL, 2001). Education coverage in Latin America has increased steadily since the 1980s. Even during periods in which poverty and inequality have risen, rates of education coverage at all levels have continued to grow. Although there is still great inequality, between different countries, as we can see in Figure 8, and within all of them, Latin America has been successful in its process of educational inclusion.

What have been the trends at different levels of education? What particularities have stood out in the last decade? Early childhood education, that is, up to three years of age, shows the lowest coverage: as of 2010, very few children have access to early development education, and only 14 per cent of two-year-olds and 35 per cent of three-year-olds have access provided by public services. However, there has been a significant increase since the beginning of the last decade, when these rates were 2 per cent and 8 per cent, respectively (Alfonso et al., 2012). Early childhood development is increasingly being recognised as vital to later acquisition of cognitive abilities. During the same period, preschool education coverage for four- and five-year-olds has nearly doubled thanks to new mandatory attendance laws for these ages in different countries, the growth of public and private educational opportunities and the rising importance placed on this phase of the education cycle by experts, governments and families.

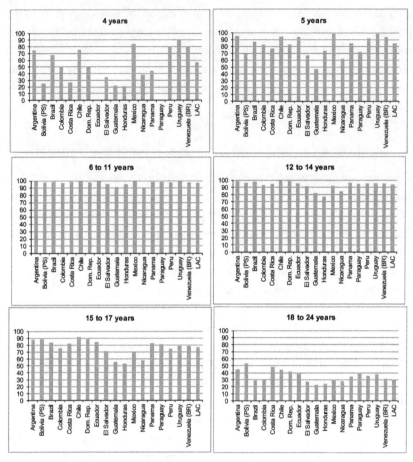

Figure 8 Latin America and the Caribbean: attendance rates by age group and country, 2013.

Source: SITEAL (2015a, 2015b, 2016)

Primary education between six and eleven years of age is mandatory in all countries and is practically universal: in the first years of the 2010s, 97.2 per cent of children between six and eleven years of age attended school (SITEAL, 2015a). Today it is considered unacceptable in all countries and social classes for a child not to attend. Since the 1980s, inclusion in primary education has increased in the countries, areas and groups in which said coverage was lagging, particularly in Central America, in rural areas and among lower classes. However, the lag in educational attainment is still a significant problem: nearly 20 per cent of children attend primary school at a grade level two years below that indicated by their age. Even so, this lag does seem to affect completion rates: in 2013, 94 per cent of Latin American adolescents between fifteen and seventeen years of age who had begun their primary education completed it. But there are still significant sectors of exclusion – for example, in Guatemala and Nicaragua, 25 per cent of those who start primary school do not finish (SITEAL, 2015a).

Secondary school is mandatory in all countries in the region, with the exception of Nicaragua: in some countries, this applies only to the first three years (twelve to fourteen years of age), whereas in others, the full cycle through seventeen years of age is compulsory. Coverage has grown constantly since the 1980s and especially during the 1990s. This rise slowed somewhat during the last decade: for some marginalised sectors, access to schooling is still severely limited. But in general, countries that were lagging behind increased their education rates in this decade. As with primary school access, there were improvements in the countries, areas and social groups that had suffered the greatest exclusion.

There are marked differences between the twelve- to fourteen-year-old age group, with 93.4 per cent attendance (2013), and the fifteen- to seventeen-year-old age group, for whom this rate drops to 76.6 per cent during the second stage. The gaps between countries are greater here than at the primary level, reaching 30 per cent: 92.1 per cent of youths between fifteen and seventeen years of age in Chile were attending school, while the same figure was only a little over 50 per cent in Honduras and Guatemala. Latin America is the only region in the developing world where there are more girls than boys at this educational level. But unlike at the primary level, entering school at the intermediate level offers no guarantee that a student will graduate: a quarter of students who begin this level do not complete it and, once again, the gaps between countries, classes and urban–rural are very high, as Table 3 shows.

With regard to secondary education, Latin America has shown an increase in coverage but experienced varying degrees of difficulty achieving an equivalent rate of completion at this level, depending on the country. D'Alessandre (2017) identifies three educational contexts: one with solid and long-term educational track records and high levels of access and completion, which includes Argentina, Chile, Bolivia and Peru; a second context with weaker trajectories in countries that combine high rates of access but low rates of completion, such as Brazil, Mexico and Uruguay, or, on the other hand, low rates of access but high rates of completion, as occurs in Panama or Paraguay; and a third context with brief and weak educational careers, in which levels of both access and completion are low, in countries like Nicaragua and Honduras. Various studies have shown that the reasons behind these trends are related to the need to work and, in the case of women, to early motherhood and the domestic workload.

Table 3 Latin America and the Caribbean: secondary school completion rate by area, per capita income quintiles and country, 2013

Country	Urban	Rural	I	II	III	IV	V
	Area		**Income quintiles**				
Argentina	53.6	–	34.0	44.9	56.1	70.8	79.0
Bolivia (PS)	65.2	43.4	–	–	–	–	–
Brazil	53.5	35.8	31.2	42.9	50.7	65.2	78.7
Chile	79.8	76.3	71.3	74.9	81.5	83.3	91.5
Colombia	56.2	34.2	34.3	43.3	53.6	62.2	69.8
Costa Rica	48.7	34.1	23.0	37.0	42.9	54.4	81.8
Ecuador	65.6	41.8	36.7	51.2	55.5	68.6	83.2
El Salvador	42.3	20.2	17.2	24.8	30.3	38.8	61.0
Guatemala	21.7	11.1	4.0	9.3	11.3	22.2	31.6
Honduras	38.5	14.8	7.5	13.3	20.6	33.5	57.6
Mexico	50.4	30.2	29.1	35.4	44.4	51.9	66.8
Nicaragua	48.5	18.3	26.1	24.6	31.8	36.7	57.9
Panama	63.3	35.5	23.2	40.4	59.5	67.2	84.7
Paraguay	59.7	33.0	25.9	36.5	45.5	62.1	72.4
Peru	82.4	58.2	54.3	71.2	80.5	86.3	92.4
Dominican Republic	52.5	42.6	34.6	39.4	46.7	53.9	74.6
Uruguay	29.2	25.7	10.1	20.2	30.7	38.5	63.5
Venezuela (BR)	–	–	57.7	67.0	66.5	74.0	74.0
LAC	**55.0**	**38.4**	**32.9**	**42.2**	**48.5**	**56.7**	**70.4**

Source: CIMA, Inter-American Development Bank

Other studies highlight a lack of interest in schooling that seems to bear little connection to youths' daily lives (Contreras & Laferte, 2017).

Finally, as for higher education, 30.8 per cent of young people between the ages of eighteen and twenty-four attended classes in 2013, and access to higher education had increased by 5 per cent since the year 2000 (SITEAL, 2016). This educational level, along with early development, has shown the most growth in the last decade. Graduation rates have increased but are still relatively low when compared to developed countries given that fewer than half of students who begin a course of study successfully complete it. The gaps between countries, and especially between different social classes within each country, are decreasing due to greater numbers of students from lower classes entering courses of higher education. There has been a general 'de-elitisation' of higher education since the 1990s (Rama, 2009). He maintains that the expansion of higher education since 1970 is comparable to the process of urbanisation between the 1940s and 1970s: in 1970, 1.6 million people between the ages of twenty and twenty-four attended a higher education institution, and in 2005, this number reached 16 million and continued to increase. It is estimated that in 2025, 65 per cent of youths will be enrolled in higher education. This increased coverage is due to pressure and demand for inclusion in higher education thanks to the expansion of secondary coverage and a greater number of employers requiring degrees as a condition for employment.

How were these advances achieved at the different levels? Mandatory attendance laws date back to the 1980s and were reinforced in the 1990s and last decade. Making education mandatory elevated its status to an enforceable right, leading to an increase in the availability of state-sponsored educational services. The demand for more education is constant: an increase in coverage at one level creates pressure for an increase in the following level. Indeed, access to education is part of social mobility processes and essential to the promise of democratisation. One trend characteristic of the new millennium has been a significant expansion of educational budgets as a percentage of GNPs, which have also grown (Cetrángolo & Curcio, 2017). Greater attention has also been given to excluded and marginalised groups, with policies aimed at their incorporation. Different countries have adopted a range of programmes and strategies to re-enrol students who have abandoned their studies, prevent dropouts and even seek out those who have not attended school in order to bring them back (Feldman, Atorresi & Mekler, 2013).

4.1.1 Is It Possible to Combine Increasing Coverage and Quality?

While the region has been successful in increasing education coverage, the same cannot be said of educational quality in general, particularly when comparisons are made to other regions and between different socio-economic classes within each country. As such, educational quality has become a central topic of current debates in the political arena, in the media and among experts.

Why is quality important? Although sufficient research has not been carried out in Latin America, there is evidence that low educational quality is detrimental to productive development and the possibility of increased productivity at work. This has led certain authors to place significant emphasis on how poor educational quality contributes to underdevelopment in the region's productive sectors (Hanushek & Woessmann, 2009). Alfonso et al. (2012) cite public opinion surveys of businesspeople in some Latin American countries showing strong dissatisfaction with the educational level of their workers and point to evidence from the US that links these gaps in learning to high levels of wage inequality (Blau & Kahn, 2006). A second question is whether quality should be measured only in terms of the production system. Those who question this maintain that the goal of education is to shape citizens and therefore that education should not be measured exclusively with regard to the supposed needs of the production system. Following from this critique, certain international studies indicate that Latin American students also show significant deficits in democratic and civic education (Cabrol & Székely, 2012).

Educational quality is measured through tests administered to students at the primary and secondary levels. In primary, there is a periodical Latin American comparative study led by the Latin American Laboratory for Assessment of the Quality of Education from UNESCO, called PERCE, SERCE and TERCE. The most important worldwide comparative test is PISA (Programme for International Student Assessment), organised by the OCDE and applied in the third year of secondary schooling (generally at the age of fifteen) in more than sixty countries around the world. In all subjects, Latin America was in the lowest one-third, and the average student only reached the lowest level of performance (Bos et al., 2012; see Figure 9). Although the situation has shown gradual improvement since the year 2000 (Rivas & Sanchez, 2016), all countries in the region (except Chile) have shown worse results than could be expected given their per capita income.

What are the causes and possible means for improving quality? First, while there have been increases in coverage, there are enormous differences in infrastructure across the region. Studies have shown high percentages of schools without electricity, internet connections, areas for teacher meetings and space for physical education or laboratories, among other shortcomings (Duarte, Gargiulo & Moreno, 2012). Second, the issue of teacher education has been raised. Teachers are poorly paid and have few years of training, and there is great resistance to the implementation of performance evaluation mechanisms. A central issue is the need to recruit best teachers, but this goal is doubtful at best since teachers' incomes are – and will likely continue to be – unappealing (Elacqua et al., 2018). There are also plans aimed at reducing differences in quality by sending greater resources to areas with the worst results, such as in Chile and Mexico (Raczynski, Wieinstein & Pascual, 2013), but they have not yet had a significant impact since the scope of such programmes is very limited.

4.1.2 Current Debates

There are other issues present in educational debates in Latin America. A central topic has been one-child-one-computer policies as a way of closing

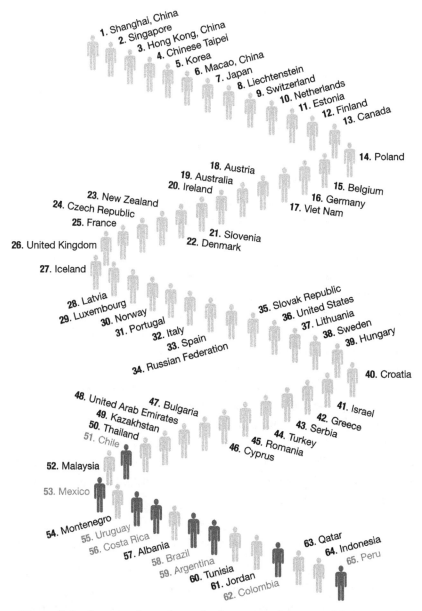

Figure 9 Performance in mathematics by country/economy. Mean score in PISA 2012 ranking. Countries and economies.

Source: OECD (2014, Table I.A)

the digital gap between classes. Distribution was successful in Uruguay, Argentina, Chile and Colombia (Rivas, 2015). Although some evaluations have been critical of the low number of hours dedicated to study with computers, these policies are a positive step with an equalising thrust (Lugo & Brito,

2015; Rivas, 2016). There is also discussion regarding the issue of school governance, with debates centring on the degree of autonomy and regulation of each institution. Indeed, after all kinds of decentralisation were favoured during the 1990s, a recentralisation of educational planning occurred in nearly all countries during the post-neo-liberal period (Malgouyres, 2014).

Since inequality and diversity were hot topics during that time, advancements were made in programmes to promote education in indigenous languages (UNICEF, 2009), include Afro–Latin American people's history and improve comprehensive sexual education – which, as could be expected, varied greatly between countries and reignited long-standing issues (World Bank, 2018). Finally, of concern across the entire region are the so-called neither-nors: youths who neither study nor work. There is perhaps excessive concern regarding this category, which, in many cases, includes a wide range of profiles (youths between jobs, mothers etc.); in any case, the spectre of a group supposedly excluded from work and education, therefore lacking a future, exacerbates existing fears of insecurity (Hoyos, Rogers & Székely, 2016).

In summary, Latin America was successful in expanding educational coverage, but quality gaps remain a growing concern. The question is if the education system today is more unequal or more equal than in the past. The answer is complex. It should be noted that we have coverage data but not quality measurements from the past. Systems were probably more homogeneous in terms of quality in the past than they are today. But it may be because those systems were more socially homogeneous given that they were more restricted in terms of coverage. Since the 1980s and 1990s, we have seen a process of inclusion of different classes at all educational levels. That is, we have a more inclusive system with probably greater internal differences than in the past, when the system was less inclusive.

4.2 Health: A Heterogeneous Epidemiological Profile

As we saw in the section on education, health and disease, indicators have also improved in the past decade. Progress has been made mainly in terms of absolute values, but significant relative inequalities and gaps continue to exist between classes, ethnic groups, countries and regions. Indeed, despite a significant increase in health spending, the region has not achieved sustained improvement in health equality, that is, in creating opportunities for all individuals to live a healthy life.

Each historical configuration of the demographic structure has a corresponding epidemiological profile for a given population. Today in Latin America, what some authors refer to as an epidemiological transition is the health-related consequence of the demographic transition to which we referred in the first section of this Element. This transition's dual profile is characterised by the coexistence of infectious diseases linked to lower stages of development, such as the persistence of infant mortality and different poverty-related illnesses. At the same time, the rate of chronic, degenerative illnesses, such as cancer and cardiovascular disease, has risen, which is to be expected as a population ages (Di Cesare, 2011). However, there is some disagreement between authors on the idea of transition; this would imply a movement from illnesses tied to lower stages of development to other types of disease, and in Latin America today, there is an overlap of both. In fact, far from disappearing, poverty-related illnesses are intensifying, and others that seemed to have been eradicated, such as cholera, are reappearing (Altagracia-Martínez et al., 2012).

This dual profile poses a challenge for health services and policies that must adapt to this heterogeneous scenario. But the conception of the population's health can also modify by new points of view, which are also not sufficiently taken into account by health services. First, there are debates on whether the health agenda should include deaths due to 'external causes' such as homicide, suicide and different types of accidents: eighteen of the twenty countries with the highest homicide rates in the world are located in Latin America and the Caribbean. For instances, while in the region the rates of traffic accidents are 31.6 per 100 000 for men and 6.9 for women, in the US they are 16.5 and 6.5, and in Canada 8.6 and 3.8, respectively. External causes have a significant impact on mortality among young people, with differences by sex. While men run a higher risk of becoming victims of homicide by a stranger, women are more likely to be murdered by a partner or to suffer other kinds of non-lethal violence at a partner's hands. The WHO (2013) indicates that in Latin America and the Caribbean, 29.8 per cent of women who have had a partner at some point have suffered physical or sexual mistreatment by a romantic partner during their lifetime. It also states that 58 per cent of children between zero and seventeen years of age suffer physical, sexual, or emotional abuse every year (Hillis et al., 2016).

Mental health also has little presence in policies despite its enormous impact on the well-being of the population (PAHO, 2009). In addition, the Latin American population is affected by the risks associated with natural disasters like hurricanes or deaths tied to environmental factors, but these issues do not have a significant place in health agendas, as is the case for accidents and occupational diseases, which cause thousands of deaths and injuries in the region (Galvão, Finkelman & Henao, 2010).

Illnesses, risks, catastrophes, diseases, violence of all kinds; their inclusion distances us from a dichotomous health-illness view of health and creates a challenge for public policy, demanding a new assessment of a society's well-being. There is also a new focus based on life course. Its two main features are taking into consideration the risk factors at each stage of the life cycle and understanding the effects over time of risks and events that occurred in previous stages (Kuh & Ben-Shlomo, 1997). As such, it places special emphasis on how the first years of life weigh on people's future health. One of its practical consequences should be different strategies by age group. For example, according to the PAHO (2017), the main causes of death by age in the Americas from 2010 to 2013 were as follows: for the ten to twenty-four age group, homicide, traffic accidents and suicide; for the twenty-five to sixty-four age group, ischaemic cardiopathy, diabetes and homicide; for the group over sixty-five years of age, ischaemic cardiopathies, cerebrovascular disease and dementia and Alzheimer's. As for the neonatal group, the main cause of death was respiratory insufficiency.

The question is whether the region's health systems are prepared to take on these new challenges. According to specialists, this is not the case, particularly because they maintain institutional attitudes arising from a traditional conception of health versus illness that cannot respond to these new profiles and regards, and these systems have not achieved equal access to health services for all people (PAHO, 2018b). In particular, services should adapt to monitor populations with different types of risks, such as diabetes, cholesterol and hypertension, through check-ups and incentives, instead of responding only by treating illnesses that have already manifested.

4.2.1 State of Health among the Population

As we have said, news in the region has been positive in the last decade if we consider aggregated data. Table 4 shows differences among countries and subregions.

Just as there have been improvements in education, the same has occurred in the field of health, and spending on health has increased as a percentage of GDP in the new millennium. As was mentioned in the first section of this Element, these years have seen a continuation of the process of decreasing mortality that began in the middle of the twentieth century. The Millennium Development Goals (MDGs) were the eight international development goals for the year 2015 that had been established following the Millennium Summit of the United Nations in 2000, after adoption of the United Nations Millennium Declaration (see ECLAC, 2015b). The PAHO indicates that life expectancy had increased to approximately seventy-five years by the period 2010–15. During the period from 2012 to 2017, the degree to which the MDGs had been achieved in Latin

Table 4 Health indicators in the Americas, circa 2015

Subregions, countries and territories	Maternal mortality ratio reported (100 000 lb)	Infant mortality rate reported (1000 lb)	Under-five mortality reported (1000 lb)	National health expenditure as percentage of GDP (2014)
The Americas	**44.2**	**13.0**	**15.8**	**5.3**
North America	**12.1**	**5.7**	**6.7**	**8.2**
Bermuda	–	3.4	3.4	–
Canada	6.1	5.0	5.8	7.4
United States of America	12.7	5.8	6.8	8.3
Latin America and the Caribbean	**58.0**	**16.1**	**19.7**	**3.7**
Latin America	**57.6**	**16.0**	**19.7**	**3.7**
Mexico	34.6	12.5	15.1	3.3
Central American Isthmus	**76.0**	**18.2**	**23.0**	**4.1**
Belize	83.2	14.3	16.5	3.9
Costa Rica	27.1	7.9	9.3	6.8
El Salvador	27.4	9.8	11.9	4.5
Guatemala	113.4	21.0	27.0	2.3
Honduras	74.0	24.0	30.0	4.4
Nicaragua	37.8	17.0	21.0	5.1
Panama	52.7	12.3	16.2	5.9
Latin Caribbean	**66.5**	**32.3**	**48.7**	**5.1**
Cuba	41.9	4.3	5.5	10.6
Dominican Republic	90.0	22.2	35.0	2.9
French Guiana	42.2	8.2	12.8	–
Guadeloupe	17.3	8.9	10.6	–
Haiti	–	59.0	88.0	1.6
Martinique	36.2	6.2	–	–
Puerto Rico	28.8	7.1	7.8	–
Andean Area	**76.2**	**18.3**	**22.1**	**3.9**
Bolivia (PS)	160.0	50.0	63.0	4.6
Colombia	53.7	17.2	19.2	5.4
Ecuador	44.6	8.9	13.9	4.5
Peru	93.0	15.0	18.0	3.3
Venezuela (BR)	68.7	14.7	16.9	1.5
Brazil	59.9	15.1	17.0	3.8
Southern Cone	**38.4**	**9.6**	**11.1**	**3.3**
Argentina	38.7	9.7	11.3	2.7
Chile	15.5	6.9	7.9	3.9
Paraguay	81.8	14.2	16.4	4.5

Table 4 (cont.)

Subregions, countries and territories	Maternal mortality ratio reported (100 000 lb)	Infant mortality rate reported (1000 lb)	Under-five mortality reported (1000 lb)	National health expenditure as percentage of GDP (2014)
Uruguay	19.1	8.0	8.7	6.1
Non-Latin Caribbean	**88.7**	**18.0**	**20.8**	**3.1**
Anguilla	–	7.1	7.1	–
Antigua and Barbuda	–	17.9	20.0	3.8
Aruba	–	4.8	–	–
Bahamas	21.3	19.9	21.9	3.6
Barbados	34.8	12.9	14.6	4.7
Cayman Islands	–	1.5	1.5	–
Curacao	–	11.2	11.7	–
Dominica	251.0	17.6	21.0	3.8
Grenada	191.6	14.7	17.9	2.8
Guyana	116.6	19.8	22.3	3.1
Jamaica	108.1	22.2	23.3	2.8
Montserrat	21.7	0.0	–	–
Saint Kitts & Nevis	155.5	23.3	23.3	2.1
Saint Lucia	98.7	16.3	16.8	3.6
Saint Vincent and the Grenadines	–	15.5	17.1	4.4
Sint Maarten (Dutch)	195.7	2.2	6.6	–
Suriname	139.8	15.9	18.5	2.9
Trinidad and Tobago	20.3	11.5	–	2.9
Turks and Caicos Islands	–	5.8	7.7	–
Virgin Islands (UK)	–	7.4	11.1	–
Virgin Islands (US)	–	–	–	–

Source: PAHO (2017)

America and the Caribbean was evaluated, revealing significant improvements in infant mortality and the attainment of a longer, healthier life. In general terms, the population of the Americas has gained an average of sixteen years of life in the last forty-five years, or nearly two years per five-year period. Between the period of 2002–5 and the period of 2010–13, maternal deaths also decreased by almost 15 per cent, and infant mortality by 24 per cent. The region achieved a 67 per cent reduction in the mortality rate of children under five years of age between 1990 and 2015. Deaths related to AIDS have also decreased by 67 per cent between 2005 and 2015 due to early retroviral treatment, although it is estimated that in 2015 there were 2 million HIV-positive people in the region (PAHO, 2017).

The above indicators somewhat obfuscate the fact that health spending has faced diminishing returns – that is, it has had less and less impact on the improvement of indicators, and as we have said, those gaps are increasing. On the one hand, there is inefficiency in expenditures, and on the other hand, health costs increase geometrically. A UNICEF report (2016) shows the persistence of great inequalities between countries, regions within countries, social classes and groups such as indigenous people (see Figure 10) with regard to birth control access, HIV infection, access to safe abortion, cancer prevention and maternal mortality and morbidity. As to the latter, the maternal mortality index is disproportionately high in the poorest countries of Latin America and the Caribbean. In 2015, 11.7 per cent of live births and 41 per cent of all maternal deaths were concentrated in the poorest countries, while these figures stood at 10.6 per cent and 8 per cent, respectively, in the richest countries during the same year. This indicator improved in absolute terms but worsened in relative terms from 2000 to 2015 because there was a greater improvement in the richest countries and among the most privileged groups in each country than among the poorest groups and countries.

The region's social heterogeneity is also made visible by the so-called emerging diseases, which in many cases were considered eradicated and are linked to poverty and extreme exclusion. These include influenza and cholera, which have been detected in Cuba, Haiti, Mexico and the Dominican Republic. There has also been an increase among so-called diseases of poverty, such as chikungunya and Zika (with more than 700 000 cases 2015–2016). Yellow fever is considered endemic in fourteen countries, and cases of dengue are also on the rise. Among neglected diseases, one of the most significant is Chagas. The PAHO estimates that there are 6 million people in the region living with this illness. All of these diseases of poverty are addressed by insufficient policies and treatment is very expensive due to laboratories' lack of interest in producing medications for a 'poor market' with little financial security (PAHO, 2017).

We must still review the other side of the dual epidemiological profile: non-communicable diseases. Currently, these are the main causes of death in the region. They are responsible for four out of five deaths every year; cardiovascular illnesses, cancer, respiratory disease and diabetes are the four leading causes of death. In fact, of all the deaths caused by these illnesses, 35 per cent were early-onset cases occurring in people of thirty to seventy years of age

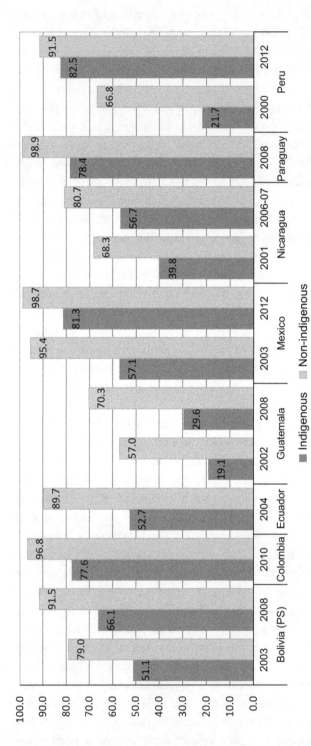

Figure 10 Latin America (eight countries): percentage of indigenous and non-indigenous women with skilled birth attendance, selected years.

Source: ECLAC (2014c)

(cancer and cardiovascular disease made up 65 per cent of these premature deaths). As we have said, their prevalence demands a modification of the health agenda to place greater importance on preventive care. Indeed, the main factors leading to these illnesses are an unhealthy diet, insufficient physical activity, tobacco use and excessive alcohol consumption. And clearly, these factors have a greater incidence as one move down the social scale.

4.2.2 Health Issues Today

What continuities and changes can be seen in Latin America during the 'post-neo-liberal shift'? With regard to public health spending, notwithstanding the great variability between countries (see Table 4) investment in health has generally increased, as has occurred with education. Twenty-two countries in the region increased their spending as a percentage of GDP between 2010 and 2014 but with a smaller increase compared to that of the previous five-year period, with the exception of Bolivia, Paraguay and Peru (PAHO, 2017). However, public spending is still insufficient: Costa Rica, Cuba and Uruguay are the only countries that assign more than 6 per cent of their GDP to public health spending (while countries such as France, Switzerland and Sweden spend more than 11 per cent). The issue is even more pressing today given that these increases occurred in a more favourable economic context than exists at present. Indeed, experts agree that the region has achieved high degrees of health coverage, which has not translated into higher levels of utilisation of preventive services, or into a reduction in barriers to access for the poor. In more general terms, if there had been access to services, 1.2 million deaths in the region would have been prevented between 2013 and 2014. An additional factor is that some countries face not only a shortage of health personnel but also a high concentration of professionals in large urban centres and few of them in less privileged areas (PAHO, 2017).

Just as education is a field of constant experimentation and change, the area of health is experiencing a kind of paradigmatic crisis due to a lack of clearly programmed guidelines or leadership at the Latin American level. As Molina and Tobar (2018) have indicated, during the neo-liberal decade of the 1990s the World Bank exercised leadership on the health agenda with its policy of privatisation, commodification and decentralisation of services. That role has not been taken up by any country in the region or by the PAHO: the discussion is somewhat lacking in leadership. Until recently, the central health debate was social determinants of health, which led many countries to create offices and state agencies, as well as programmes to deal with this issue. Strictly speaking, this is a paradigm that dates from the 1970s and was the product of a review of mortality and morbidity factors. Four determinants were established: genetics, environment, lifestyle and health systems, and it was estimated that each was responsible for a portion of mortality and morbidity (Galvão, Finkelman & Henao, 2010). What was new about this approach was that it took centrality away from health services and showed how each of the above factors weight on health and illness. This approach would have led to a radical change in health policy, as occurred to an extent in Europe, by leading governments to focus on policies to improve lifestyles and environments and pay more attention to genetic factors. This did not occur, although there was a moderate impact on the agenda of topics and new problems. The transition from neo-liberalism to a different political phase has also failed to lead to a paradigmatic change in health. Two systems which did experience far-reaching reform, albeit during the neo-liberal period, were those of Chile and Colombia (Laurell, 2016). These were considered 'pro-market' reforms which increased private spending. The subsequent 'reform of the reform' in Chile included corrections that led to improvements in terms of equality (for the Chilean case, see Urriola et al., 2016).

What changes can be seen in recent years? Aside from the increase in social spending, other new and positive measures were taken during this period. One achievement was the establishment of certain types of insurance for previously uncovered sectors of the population, as in Mexico and Peru. Likewise, the concept of explicit health guarantees (EHGs) became more widespread. EHGs are provisions in the law mandating that certain services must be available to the entire population at a minimum standard of quality. They exist in some countries in the region, particularly in Uruguay, Peru and Ecuador. However, the degree to which these policies translate into actual provision of care remains to be evaluated.

A second change are related to 'catastrophic illnesses', a group of different diseases, some very rare and others more common, which together affect millions of people. They are catastrophic due to their extremely high cost, impossible to take on for the majority of families that suffer from them, and also because they can destabilise health insurance. There have been efforts to address catastrophic illnesses through different types of insurance, funding or state provision of medications in countries such as Uruguay, Argentina, El Salvador and the Dominican Republic. Also the political agenda is currently focused on the concept of universal health coverage (Atun et al., 2015), but the truth is that many countries do not agree on what this means in real terms due to its economic costs: as the coverage becomes more 'universal', more services should, at least in theory, be provided to the population.

As to the problems faced by health systems, as mentioned above, the main issue is the inability to provide equitable access to health care. This occurs in a context of growing spending due to the constant increase in the population's health demands to meet the care needs of an ageing population and, more recently, due to technological advancements. Indeed, medications and treatments are increasingly expensive despite their sometimes modest impact in extending life, sometimes only by a few short years. The demand for these newer drugs is often played out in the legal system, usually by those users with the resources to pursue lawsuits. This has led to criticism that the transfer of health issues to the legal system favours the promotion of inequality rather than equality and leads to a lack of rationality in systems (Vidal & Di Fabio, 2017). This is exacerbated by the fact that weak and fragmented health systems like those in Latin America have little pull with powerful international laboratories when negotiating the prices of drugs, equipment or treatments, unlike in centralised European systems, such as those of France or Great Britain.

In summary, health indicators improve across Latin America, but in some of those, inequality among countries and within them increased. But the epidemiological profile is also changing. Although there is expanded access to basic health services, many treatments and medications have fallen outside the reach of low-income populations due to the care needs of an ageing population and technology advances. But compared to education, health issues are less visible in the public conversation.

4.3 Housing: The Persistence of Old Problems

As in the case of health and education, Latin America has shown improvements with regard to housing during the first decade of this century. Following previous trends, there was a reduction during these years in the percentage of households with housing problems. However, since the population has grown, there has been hardly any change in absolute terms. The region continues to face problems related to the characteristics of neighbourhoods and cities that affect the well-being of the population and create inequality of life opportunities.

Latin America has historically been characterised by a lack of ability to adequately house its entire population. In cities, the problem worsened in the second half of the twentieth century, during the years of high rural–urban migration and accelerated urbanisation discussed in the first section of the Element. States with little capacity for planning and investment were faced with a marked increase in demand for housing and services by (mostly low-income) families arriving in the cities. As a result, urban expansion in Latin America occurred in a disorganised manner with significant housing deficits.

One of its distinctive features was the multiplication of informal neighbour-hoods generally created from irregular occupation of land and self-built housing. In Rio de Janeiro, for example, the percentage of people living in *favelas* and other informal settlements increased from 10 per cent to more than 20 per cent between 1961 and 2009. The increase in absolute numbers was from 300 000 to 1.25 million (Bouillon, 2012).

Currently, the deceleration in urban growth seen in many countries in the region has taken pressure off the demand for housing and services, creating an opportunity to focus efforts on improving what already exists. UN-Habitat (2012) proposed that Latin America is in a position to experience a new urban transition, this time oriented towards improving quality of life in cities. However, other socio-demographic changes, related to the structure of house-holds, have the opposite effect on the demand for housing. Recent trends such as an increase in single-person or single-parent households are bringing about a reduction in average household sizes, implying a greater demand for housing. These changes also affect the design of housing and public spaces; an ageing population creates the challenge of planning cities that consider the needs of the elderly.

What are the main problems faced by the region today with regard to housing? Authors usually differentiate between quantitative housing defi-cits, which measure a lack in the stock of housing units, and qualitative ones, which include housing that does not meet minimum standards of habitability. According to IDB data from 2009 for eighteen countries (Table 5), the percentage of urban households in the region with some kind of habitability deficit is 32 per cent. The majority, 26 per cent, have qualitative deficits: insecurity of tenure, inadequate materials, lack of drink-ing water, lack of adequate sewerage and overcrowding. The main problems identified were the lack of sewerage (13 per cent) and insecurity of tenure (11 per cent), while a lower percentage of households live in housing built from inadequate materials (7 per cent), lack drinking water (6 per cent), suffer from overcrowding (4 per cent) and have no access to electricity (1 per cent).

However, the situation varies greatly from country to country. On one end of the spectrum are countries where half or more of urban households face some kind of habitability problem: Nicaragua (70 per cent), Bolivia (64 per cent), Peru (60 per cent), Guatemala (57 per cent) and El Salvador 49 per cent). On the other end, Costa Rica (12 per cent), Chile (19 per cent) and Uruguay (25 per cent) show the best relative situation (Table 6). And, as might be expected, there are significant differences with regard to the income level of households. While those in the top quintile, with the highest income, experience

Table 5 Latin America and the Caribbean: housing deficits by area and per capita income quintiles, 2009 (percentage of households)

Housing deficits	Total	Area		Income quintiles				
		Urban	Rural	I	II	III	IV	V
Total	37	32	60	52	39	32	24	16
Quantitative shortages	6	6	5	9	8	6	5	3
Qualitative shortages	31	26	55	43	31	26	19	12
Materials	12	7	32	16	10	6	4	2
Dirt floors	6	2	22	5	3	2	1	0
Poor roof	3	2	6	3	2	2	1	1
Poor walls	2	1	6	2	1	1	0	0
Overcrowding	6	4	13	10	6	3	2	0
Infrastructure	21	16	43	30	20	16	10	6
Lack electricity	4	1	17	2	1	1	0	0
Lack sanitation	15	13	27	25	16	12	7	4
Lack piped water	9	6	20	11	7	6	4	3
Lack of secure tenure	11	11	15	16	12	10	9	6

Source: Bouillon (2012, Table 2.2)

a total deficit of 16 per cent, among the poorest households in the first quintile, the percentage is 3.3 times higher at 52 per cent (Table 5).

A first review of the recent evolution of the housing situation reveals a heartening outlook: in relative terms, housing problems have decreased. According to IDB data (Bouillon, 2012), between 1995 and 2009, the percentage of households with some quantitative or qualitative deficit decreased, with the exception of insecurity of tenure. It is also noteworthy that the greatest improvement was among the poorest households, which led to a reduction in inequality between different income levels. However, the same data show that during these years, there was no improvement in absolute terms: as the region's population grew, the number of households with deficits remained the same or even increased.

The information on the urban population living in slums shows similar trends. This indicator – used to monitor one of the MDGs – covers similar shortages to those included in the measurement of qualitative deficits (housing without access to drinking water, without sewerage, with overcrowding and/or

Table 6 Urban housing deficits in Latin America and the Caribbean by country, 2009 (percentage of households)

Country	Quantitative shortages	Qualitative shortages				
		Total	Materials	Over crowding	Infrastructure	Lack of secure tenure
Argentina	5	27	9	6	13	16
Bolivia (PS)	30	34	27	23	32	11
Brazil	6	25	2	0	22	7
Chile	3	16	1	1	2	14
Colombia	9	19	7	4	9	10
Costa Rica	2	10	5	1	1	6
Dominican Republic	3	32	5	3	25	9
Ecuador	10	31	14	8	19	13
Guatemala	11	46	32	27	32	10
Honduras	2	41	18	14	26	12
Mexico	2	26	9	5	8	15
Nicaragua	12	58	33	28	52	10
Panama	8	29	7	6	22	13
Peru	14	46	34	11	29	21
Paraguay	3	36	13	9	25	10
El Salvador	8	41	21	16	30	17
Uruguay	0	25	4	3	4	22
Venezuela (BR)	8	20	13	6	5	6

Source: Bouillon (2012, Table 2.4)

built with inadequate materials). Data from the United Nations show that the percentage of urban households living in slums dropped from 34 per cent in 1990 to 29 per cent in 2000, and to 21 per cent in 2014. The region is also in a better situation relative to others in the developing world: with the exception of Northern Africa (11 per cent), the percentage of the population living in slums in Latin America (21 per cent) is lower than that in different regions of Asia (between 25 per cent and 31 per cent), in Oceania (24 per cent) or in sub-Saharan Africa (55 per cent).

The greater coverage of services like electricity, water or sewerage does not necessarily imply that such services are provided in adequate conditions. For example, it is estimated that some 25 per cent of access to drinking water takes place through informal or illegal means and that in many households, especially poor ones, drinking water is only available a few hours a day. In Tegucigalpa,

Honduras, about 80 per cent of the richest households have drinking water for more than eight hours a day, while among the poorest households, that proportion is 50 per cent (UN-Habitat, 2012).

In addition, information on housing improvements says nothing about what happens in the broader environment. Housing is much more than four walls and a roof, which is why growing attention has been paid to other aspects that have a strong influence on people's quality of life, such as the location and security of a neighbourhood, provision of services and infrastructure, access to facilities and urban form and density. In all these areas, the region has significant progress to make.

First, informal neighbourhoods, where most deficient housing is concentrated, are still a distinctive feature of cities in the region. It is true that there have been improvements and, in particular, a change in public policy. While in the past policy towards informal neighbourhoods was characterised by forced evictions, in the last two decades there has been a shift towards acceptance. In general terms, evictions have ceased, and initiatives to legalise and improve informal settlements have been prioritised. However, the numbers of households that live in this kind of neighbourhood is still high, and continue to face problems such as a lack of development and illegality. While the expansion of marginal neighbourhoods in Latin America goes back several decades, recent studies have focused on what is happening with the second generation of inhabitants (Ward, Jiménez & Di Virgilio, 2014). Studies show that long-standing irregular tenure leads to difficulties in the inheritance or sale of housing, and the corresponding ability to capitalise on its accumulated value.

Cities in Latin America are also characterised by urban segregation, the concentration of households that share similar social conditions (socio-economic, ethnic) in the same neighbourhoods or areas of the city. The best example of this phenomenon is the contrast between marginal neighbourhoods, where the lowest-income population is concentrated, and gated communities, isolated from the rest of the city by walls or fences, which expanded in the region during the last decades of the twentieth century and are inhabited by upper-middle-class and upper-class households. Spatial segregation has serious implications for the well-being and life opportunities of the population. Inequality in Latin America is, in this sense, 'socio-territorial' (Di Virgilio & Perelman, 2014). Cities' poor populations live in areas with fewer services, public spaces and green spaces; they are further from transportation, commercial areas and work opportunities and in general face higher levels of insecurity and violence.

Studies on urban mobility, an issue that has received increasing attention in recent years, clearly illustrate the negative effects of territorial inequalities on the population's daily lives. People with lower incomes must travel greater distances and spend more time on their daily commutes through the city, and they do so in less comfortable conditions than their higher-income counterparts. In Montevideo, the time spent on daily commutes by the higher classes is twenty-eight minutes on the average, while lower classes spend an average of forty-three minutes commuting (Mauttone & Hernández, 2017). Studies in other cities show that the most privileged groups not only live closer to their jobs but also make more frequent use of cars for commuting, in contrast to the poorer classes, who depend more on public transportation (CAF, 2010).

Other problems in the region are linked to the way in which urban growth occurs. In recent decades, Latin American cities grew in a less compact fashion, drastically increasing urban sprawl. As spatial expansion of cities has outstripped population growth, per capita land use has increased: in Buenos Aires, for example, the figure rose from 126 to 140 metres per person between 1990 and 2015; in Mexico City, it rose from 106 to 119 metres; in Santiago de Chile, from 102 to 118; and in Quito, from 110 to 185 (Montero & García, 2017). Low urban density is strongly linked to the pattern of urban expansion in the region, which occurs in a disorganised and unplanned manner towards the peripheries. This trend has in fact intensified in recent years by a process that involves different social classes, as shown by the development of gated communities for higher-income households or the construction of state-subsidised housing for poor classes in peripheral areas (UN-Habitat, 2012).

The way in which urban expansion occurs has several negative consequences. For one, the lack of planning and comprehensive vision can worsen segregation and its effects on inequality of life opportunities. Low-density growth is also both unsustainable in environmental terms and economically inefficient – the network of infrastructure and services must broaden its coverage to ever more distant areas, and the cost per inhabitant increases as population density decreases.

4.3.1 Housing Policy

What were the main housing policies during this period? How did they respond to the trends just described? In general, there were no great innovations in policy type, and, as the indicators show, little has been done to counteract socio-spatial segregation and other problematic features of urban growth. As in past periods, policies have concentrated on the construction of housing which, as we have seen, contributed to a significant reduction in housing deficits. Indeed, the turning point in policy occurred in Chile in the 1970s, when the state transferred its role as builder of social housing to private companies. Then, instead of building, it began to provide funding to facilitate access to housing for low-income classes. In general, subsidies were promoted through a so-called ABC model (*ahorro, bono y crédito*, or 'savings, subsidy and credit'), which expanded access to housing for low-income households through a combination of different types of facilities.

This period differed from previous ones due to the introduction of a very significant increase in public budgets. Studies show that at least Argentina, Mexico, Chile, Brazil and Colombia had important national programmes for housing construction through private companies. Some noteworthy programmes were Minha casa minha vida in Brazil and a series of programmes funded by INFONAVIT (National Fund for Housing for Workers, or Fondo Nacional de Vivienda para los Trabajadores) in Mexico.

These policies have been the object of a series of criticisms and controversies. In general, the quality of housing is questioned, and it is argued that local governments do not create urban infrastructure, such as services and transportation, in new, often distant settlements and that policies are aimed at middle- or low-income households but do not benefit the poorest. Ruprah (2010) shows that housing loan repayment amounts can increase poverty and homelessness by surpassing the financial capacity of low-income families. And since the first housing policies of this kind were introduced in Chile, there has been criticism of the type of urbanisation created: low-quality houses in isolated areas, increasing the disconnection between the poor and opportunities in the city. As such, families can access housing only at the cost of increased socio-spatial segregation and isolation. Over the last decade, an important debate has taken place on the best way to resolve these issues, albeit without much success. Social housing policies have not met the need for integrated cities. More housing does not equal city integration, and though housing policy should always incorporate an urban dimension and specific actions, this is not always the case.

The central issue is land access. This problem has not been resolved and, in a sense, has grown worse in the post-neo-liberal period as a result of generalised economic reactivation. In fact, urban and rural land has become much more expensive in the last decade due to public investment, urban development and the expansion of agricultural boundaries. Ultimately, when the private sector is the main actor, its interests will lead it to build on cheap land far from cities and with little connection to them. One of the contradictions of this period was the existence of housing development policies without land regulation policies. Experts agree on the need for 'capital gains recovery' policies as a means for repaying the increase in value of private land generated by public investments like, for example, new roads. Property taxes are traditionally low in Latin

America and the Caribbean, where they only represent 0.37 per cent of the region's GDP, compared to 2.12 per cent in OECD countries (Uribe & Bejarano, 2009). Only during the last decade has the region begun to implement mechanisms to recapture land values, such as impact or improvement taxes, specifically because these funds would help to cover the costs of investments in infrastructure. However, very little progress has been made in this sense.

One question is whether public policies have contributed to improving rates of informality in cities, which is perhaps the central issue in Latin American metropolitan centres. The improvement in housing deficits has of course had a positive impact on informal cities. However, overall evaluations are not very optimistic. Informality has grown in many cities in the region due to the high cost of land and housing, as well as increases in the population living in poverty. As mentioned above, common criticisms point out that subsidy policies do not generally include the poorest part of the population, but also that national policies are not aligned with sub-national actions, in order to achieve results that satisfy residents. This has led, as discussed, to a gradual abandonment of relocation policies; today's overarching goal is for the informal city to become part of the formal city. This implies improving local services, and especially enhancing connections with the rest of the city where distance is an issue. In particular, there are problems surrounding participation by the communities who are the main stakeholders in these policies, a situation leading to numerous conflicts in different countries. Nonetheless, one positive aspect of the period is the promotion of mechanisms for participation, such as cooperatives in Uruguay and community participation in Brazil and Argentina. However, given the volume of the housing deficit, few countries can truly aspire to achieve universalisation of decent housing in the short or medium term.

Finally, one series of issues stands out as important despite receiving little space on agendas: policies on leasing housing, of particular interest to low-income populations, the elderly and people who live alone. Renting a home is extremely expensive for the poor, and because they often do not meet minimum formal requirements, they must use the informal market, where they pay even more. In many cases, renting becomes an option, instead of owning a distant house, because the rent money allows to live closer to the centre of the city. However, to date this issue has largely been left off the agenda in the region. A key topic is the existence of policies to improve qualitative deficits, that is, improvements to existing homes. Infrastructure policies and subsidies have contributed to overcoming some of these problems, but the truth is that qualitative deficits vary widely: some cases demand a reduction of overcrowding, while others reflect a need for greater connection to services, or general maintenance. The most effective policies are subsidies enabling the owners themselves to take on the specific improvements required for each home. But the limited access experienced by low-income populations is a major problem, especially for those in the informal labour market for whom it is impossible to access the formal financial system.

So, it appears that the need for comprehensive urban planning policies that affect living conditions for the entire population – transportation, security, waste disposal, the environment etc. – is central to improving the housing outlook in Latin America. Urban planning policies require bringing together a large number of public and private actors, experts and members of different social organisations. Evaluations highlight that these efforts have not been particularly successful, especially because there is little incentive for participation and coordination of a multitude of actors on a long-term basis.

In summary, urban issues are of fundamental importance in a highly urbanised region, and without a doubt, they have been and will continue to be one of the most important demands of the period. This issue has been the focus of significant conflict concerning the best way to promote communities' involvement in decisions affecting their own living conditions, and because of the high cost of policies and the diversity of interests involved. And, as we have seen, policies are still focused mainly on construction, giving insufficient attention to other housing and urban issues discussed above, in particular a growing socio-spatial segregation.

4.4 Summary

What are the common and specific features in the areas of health, education and housing in the region? As we said, it has been a period of improvements in each of these spheres. In education, coverage at different stages has increased; in health, mortality and morbidity indicators have improved; and in housing, quantitative and qualitative deficits have been reduced. This occurred during a period of economic reactivation and increased social spending by governments. But we also see that in many cases, positive trends in indicators, especially regarding health and education, had already begun earlier. In a period of economic boom and social investment, these favourable trends should intensify.

However, shortages and significant deficits remain in all areas, and inequalities persist both between countries and within them. In some cases, absolute indicators have improved, but relative inequalities remain because more privileged countries or sectors have experienced the same or greater improvement than poorer countries or social groups. In particular, there was at the same time more coverage in education, health and improvement in housing, but persistent quality differences among services can access different classes and social groups.

Each dimension holds its own trajectories and tensions, which exhibit at the same time the increase of coverage and the differences in the quality of services and new faces of inequality. In education the continuous increase of overage in general went hand in hand with increasing quality gaps between social groups. With regard to health, there has been an increase in public and private spending, but it has not achieved guaranteed access to services for the poorest sectors. Diseases of poverty continue to be an issue, and the increased cost of health indicates that inequalities will be maintained or worsen over time. More and more treatments and medications have fallen outside the reach of low-income populations due to the care needs of an ageing population and technology advances. In housing, there have been improvements, but economic reactivation and urban and rural expansion have raised the price of land, and spatial segregation has become more visible.

5 Has Latin American Society Changed?

This Element tried to answer the following questions: How was the trajectories of Latin American societies in the twenty-first century? What is Latin America like today and how does this compare to the past? What has changed in the social structure of the region in recent decades and, particularly, in the new millennium? We have considered key variables of the social structure of Latin America, including demographics, family, income, education, health and housing. In this final section, we provide an overview of all the areas analysed to revisit the argument that have guided our discussion.

Our argument was that despite changes in public policies at the turn of the millennium, that increased the overall welfare of the population, Latin American societies continue to be structurally unequal in terms of class, gender and ethnicity. The improvement in welfare was the result of both public policies, such as conditional cash transfers, and a long-standing trend of reduced mortality and fertility, which started in the mid twentieth century. The growth in health and education coverage, as well as improvements in housing had also contributed to improve the welfare of the population, but with increasing differences in the quality of the services that different social groups can access and new forms of inequality emerged. Therefore, more than a decrease in inequalities, there was a decrease in the more extreme forms of exclusion.

We showed that there have been changes in each area, but the scope of these transformations – and their timing – has varied. For instance, Latin American societies underwent intense processes of urbanisation and are no longer predominantly rural: in 1950, four out of ten Latin Americans lived in cities; that figure is now eight out of ten. Life expectancy at birth rose from fifty-one years in 1950 to seventy-four years at present, and Latin Americans currently suffer and die from different diseases than they did decades earlier. In 2015, the fertility rate was 2.1 births per woman, while this figure was nearly 3 times higher in 1960, at 5.9. Women have increasingly joined the labour market and, even more so, the education system, where they now represent the majority. They have thereby modified their daily activities, projects, expectations and, to a certain degree, their conjugal relationships and roles within the family. Access to formal education has shown constant improvement: primary education is almost universal, secondary education is available for the majority of the population and access to higher education has increased steadily in recent decades. Compared to the 1950s, there is a lower rate of deficient housing, which is defined as that without access to public utilities. As such, we can maintain that Latin American society is more urban, enjoys greater longevity, stays in education longer and suffers from less gender inequality than in the past.

We also address the question of changes during the last decade. The first novelty was the drop on income inequality due to improvements in the labour market and the extension of cash transfers. The second one was the increasing coverage in education, health and improvements in housing. The political agenda during the post-neo-liberal period focused on alleviating the most extreme forms of exclusion created during the last decades of the twentieth century. Policies on housing, health, education, income and labour contributed to a safety net and minimum well-being standards for the least privileged groups. The state played a central role in this transformation not because of the novel nature of the policies implemented, as there was little innovation in this regard, but rather due to the depth and breadth of their application in diverse areas, and to the integration of labour protection policies. Certainly, the most ground-breaking aspect was a considerable broadening of welfare payments to the poorest sectors of society (through conditional cash transfer programmes and old-age pensions).

However, there are still significant issues of exclusion within each country, and past problems remain. There are social groups with no access to basic education; informal settlements are still a distinctive feature of cities in the region; and certain illnesses associated with poverty are on the rise, while others which were considered to have been eradicated have reappeared. These social problems are concentrated among the poor, the indigenous population, those of African descent and rural dwellers. While some social groups progressed, others remain highly vulnerable. This is the case of informal workers or beneficiaries of conditional cash transfers who could see their quality of life deteriorate once again if the economic or political context changes.

So, what has happened in terms of the reduction of inequality, the great promise of the post-neo-liberal decade? It is true that in comparison to the neo-liberal years, inequality has shrunk, as seen throughout the Element. However, the first decade of the twenty-first century was characterised by a reduction in exclusion rather than a real improvement in terms of equality. First, in general terms, governments did not alter the structural foundations of persistent inequality. There was almost no transformation in production structures, or a substantial change in the relationship between capital and work, for example through progressive agrarian or tax reform. In fact, although the numbers of the poor decreased during the first decade of the century, the elites grew richer. Second, many indicators of health, education and housing improved in absolute terms, but gaps between the rich and poor generally did not decrease. This is because in many cases, the most privileged countries and groups saw greater advancement than did the poorest. Therefore, the socio-economic indicators improved, and nearly all groups experienced progress during the period. We can therefore question the notion of whether real progress was made in terms of equality. In our view, the post-neo-liberal period managed to achieve the unfulfilled promise of the social policies of the neo-liberal period with relative success, creating a basic safety net for the most excluded sectors more than a real change in terms of persistent inequalities.

Secondly, inequality has taken on new forms. Latin America has been successful at expanding education coverage, but social inclusion seems to have come hand in hand with a higher range in the quality of education. Housing deficits have been reduced, but spatial segregation has become more visible. Although there is expanded access to basic health services, many treatments and medications have fallen outside the reach of low-income populations due to the care needs of an ageing population and technology advances.

5.1 Policy and Social Change

What, then, has been the role of policy in these changes? On the one hand, it has contributed to transformations. Historically, education, health and housing policy and, more recently, broader income coverage had played a part in the current configuration of Latin American society. We maintain, however, that part of this change can be attributed to society's new image of itself. Population ageing, changes in epidemiological profiles, the quality of education, socio-spatial segregation, teen pregnancy and population care requirements are not necessarily recent trends, but until a few decades ago they were not viewed as issues deserving policy attention. To what extension policies have taken into consideration these changes? Population ageing implies challenges for the pension system, the health care system and urban design. The demographic dividend is an opportunity for countries but requires adequate planning. More inclusive education creates a need for innovation in teaching. Reading the sections of this Element, one could conclude that policy has not kept pace with society's structural modifications. Whether due to economic restrictions, path-dependence or a lack of incentives for action in the medium term, policy is clearly trailing behind certain changes.

There is also uncertainty as to the actual repercussions of some of the transformations that have taken place. This can be attributed, in part, to unexpected outcomes. The increase in school enrolment, for example, did not lead to a transformation in the production structure or strong growth in productivity or democratic values. Contrary to theories that link economic hardship with delinquency, crime rates rose in Latin America during this period of reactivation, due in part to the greater circulation of goods and money (Bergman, 2018). In fact, positive changes in certain areas can have negative consequences in others. Economic reactivation and the greater demand for agricultural goods, for example, pushed up prices of rural and urban real estate, further complicating access to housing among the poor. In addition, rising debt among low-income groups has been one of the consequences of the consumption boom of the new century. It is therefore necessary to examine the way we think about different kinds of social change and their implications.

This brings us to a central concern in Latin America today: how sustainable are the changes that have occurred, given the current context? The period of prosperity has passed, and there has been a political shift to the right in several countries accompanied by conservative reactions in society regarding gender, race and progress for low-income groups. We wish to emphasise the fact that the changes presented in this Element are critical to analysing the potential for popular resistance to efforts among conservatives to limit people's rights and undermine the social progress made in the previous period.

This Element comes to a close at a moment of change for the region. Latin American society has undergone a deep transformation, one that perhaps exceeds economic changes or those in other areas more widely studied by social scientists, such as policy. These social changes must be considered important variables when analysing political, economic or cultural phenomena. We hope that this Element has made a contribution by offering an up-to-date overview of our society, which has metamorphosised and continues to change every day.

References

Alfonso, M., Bos, M. S., Duarte, J. & Rondon, C. (2012). Panorama general de la educación en América Latina y el Caribe. In M. Cabrol & M. Székely (eds.), *Educación para la Transformación*. Washington, DC: Inter-American Development Bank, pp. 1–52.

Altagracia-Martínez, M., Kravzov-Jinich, J., Moreno-Bonett, C., López-Naranjo, F. & Martínez-Núñez, J. M. (2012). Las enfermedades 'olvidadas' de América Latina y el Caribe: un problema de salud pública global. *Revista mexicana de ciencias farmacéuticas*, 43(1), pp. 33–41. www.scielo.org.mx/scielo.php?script=sci_arttext&pid=S1870-01952012000100004&lng=es&tlng=es.

Alvaredo, F. & Gasparini, L. (2015). Recent trends in inequality and poverty in developing countries. In A. Atkinson & F. Bourguignon (eds.), *Handbook of Income Distribution*, vol. 2. London: Elsevier, pp. 697–805.

Alvaredo, F. & Londoño V. J. (2014). Altos ingresos e impuesto de renta en Colombia, 1993–2010. *Revista de Economía Institucional*, 16(31), pp. 157–94.

Alvaredo, F. & Piketty, T. (2010). The dynamics of income concentration in developed and developing countries: A view from the top. In L. F. López-Calva & N. Lustig (eds.), *Declining Inequality in Latin America: A Decade of Progress*. Baltimore, MD: Brookings Institution Press, pp. 72–99.

Amarante, V. & Arim, R. (2015). *Desigualdad e informalidad en América Latina: Un análisis de cinco experiencias latinoamericanas*. Santiago de Chile: CEPAL.

Amarante, V. & Brun, M. (2018). Cash transfers in Latin America: Effects on poverty and redistribution. *Economía Journal*, (1), pp. 1–31.

Amarante, V. & Colacce, M. (2018). ¿Más o menos desiguales? Una revisión sobre la desigualdad de los ingresos a nivel global, regional y nacional. *Revista CEPAL*, 124, pp. 7–34.

Arellano Cueva, R. (2010). Valores e ideología. El comportamiento político y económico de las nuevas clases medias en América Latina. In A. Bárcena & N. Serra (eds.), *Clases medias y desarrollo en América Latina*. Santiago de Chile: CEPAL-CIDOB, pp. 201–36.

Ariza, M. & de Oliveira, O. (2008). Familias, pobreza y desigualdad social en Latinoamérica: una mirada comparativa. *Revista Latinoamericana de Población*, 1(2), pp. 73–98.

Atun, R., De Andrade, L. O. M., Almeida, G., Cotlear, D., Dmytraczenko, T., Frenz, P., Garcia, P., Gómez-Dantés, O., Knaul, F., Muntaner, C., De Paula, J.

B., Rígoli, F., Serrate, P.C.F. & Wagstaff, A. (2015). Health-system reform and universal health coverage in Latin America. *The Lancet*, 385(9974), pp. 1230–47.

Beaton, K., Cerovic, S., Galdamez, M., Hadzi-Vaskov, M., Loyola, F., Koczan, Z., Lissovolik, B., Martijn, J., Ustyugova, Y. & Wong, J. (2017). *Migration and Remittances in Latin America and the Caribbean: Engines of Growth and Macroeconomic Stabilizers?* IMF Working Paper 144. Washington, DC: International Monetary Fund.

Beccaria, L. A. (2016). América Latina en los 2000s: aspectos laborales y distributivos. *Ciência & Trópico*, 40(2), pp. 29–58.

Bergman, M. (2018). *More Money, More Crime: Prosperity and Rising Crime in Latin America*. Oxford: Oxford University Press.

Bértola, L. & Williamson, J. (eds.) (2017). *Has Latin American Inequality Changed Direction? Looking Over the Long Run*. New York: Springer.

Birdsall, N. (2007). *Reflections on the Macro Foundations of the Middle Class in the Developing World*. Center for Global Development Working Paper 130. Washington, DC: Center for Global Development.

Birdsall, N., Lustig, N. & Meyer, C. J. (2014). The strugglers: The new poor in Latin America? *World Development*, 60, pp. 132–46.

Blau, F. & Kahn, L. (2006). The U.S. gender pay gap in the 1990s: Slowing convergence. *Industrial and Labor Relations Review*, 60(1), pp. 45–66. http://ideas.repec.org/a/ilr/articl/v60y2006i1p45-66.html.

Blofield, M. & Luna, J. P. (2011). Public opinion on income inequalities in Latin America. In M. Blofield (ed.), *The Great Gap: Inequality and the Politics of Redistribution in Latin America*. University Park: Penn State Press, pp. 147–81.

Bos, M. S., Ganimian, A. & Vegas, E. (2012), *Pisa 2012: como le fue a la region?* Washington, DC: BID.

Bouillon, C. P. (2012). *Room for Development: Housing Markets in Latin America and the Caribbean*. Washington, DC: Inter-American Development Bank.

Burdín, G., Esponda, F. & Vigorito, A. (2014). *Inequality and Top Incomes in Uruguay: A Comparison between Household Surveys and Income Tax Microdata*. CEQ Working Paper No. 21. Louisiana: Center for InterAmerican Policy and Research and Department of Economics, Tulane University.

Cabella, W. & Pardo, I. (2014). Hacia un régimen de baja fecundidad en América Latina y el Caribe, 1990–2015. In S. Cavenaghi & W. Cabella (eds.), *Comportamiento reproductivo y fecundidad en América Latina: una agenda inconclusa*. Río de Janeiro: ALAP, pp. 13–31.

Cabrol, M. & Székely, M. (2012). Introducción. ¿Cómo lograr una transformación posible? In M. Cabrol & M.Székely (eds.), *Educación para la Transformación.* Washington, DC: Inter-American Development Bank, pp. v–xxvii.

CAF (2010). *Observatorio de Movilidad Urbana para América Latina.* Caracas: CAF. http://scioteca.caf.com/handle/123456789/420.

Castellani, F., Parent, G. & Zenteno, J. (2014). *The Latin American Middle Class: Fragile After All?* IDB Working Paper 557. Washington, DC: Inter-American Development Bank.

CELADE-UNFPA (2005). *Dinámica demográfica y desarrollo en América Latina y el Caribe.* Serie Población y Desarrollo 58. Santiago de Chile: CEPAL.

CEMLA (2016). *Las remesas hacia América Latina y el Caribe en 2015–2016. Acelerando su crecimiento.* México, DF: CEMLA.

Centeno, M. A. & Portes, A. (2006). The informal economy in the shadow of the state. In *Out of the Shadows: Political Action and the Informal Economy in Latin America.* University Park, Pa: Pennsylvania State University Press, pp. 23–48.

Cerrutti, M. & Bertoncello, R. (2006). Urbanization and internal migration patterns in Latin America. In E. Preston-Whyte, M. Tienda, S. Findley & S. Tollman (eds.), *Africa on the Move: African Migration and Urbanization in Comparative Perspective.* Johannesburg: Witwatersrand University Press, pp. 141–156.

Cerrutti, M. & Binstock, G. (2009). *Familias latinoamericanas en transformación: desafíos y demandas para la acción pública.* Serie Políticas Sociales 147. Santiago de Chile: CEPAL.

Cetrángolo, O. & Curcio, J. (2017). *Financiamiento y gasto educativo en América Latina.* Santiago de Chile: Ministerio de Asuntos Exteriores de Noruega-CEPAL.

Chackiel, J. (2004). *La dinámica demográfica en América Latina.* Serie Población y Desarrollo 52. Santiago de Chile: CEPAL.

Cienfuegos, J. (2014). Tendencias familiares en América Latina: diferencias y entrelazamientos. *Notas de población,* 99, pp. 11–36.

Contreras, D. & Lafferte, M. (2017). La dimensión subjetiva de los procesos de desescolarización. Debate actual sobre representaciones sociales e identidad en la relación entre los jóvenes y la escuela secundaria. In N. López, R. Opertti & C. Vargas Tamez (eds.), *Adolescentes y jóvenes en realidades cambiantes. Notas para repensar la educación secundaria en América Latina.* París: UNESCO, pp. 41–62.

Cornia, G. (ed.) (2014). *Falling Inequality in Latin America: Policy Changes and Lessons.* Oxford: Oxford University Press.

Cortés, R. & Marshall, A. (1999). Estrategia económica, instituciones y negociación política en la reforma social de los noventa. *Desarrollo Económico,* 39(154), pp. 195–212.

D'Alessandre, V. (2017). La relación de las y los jóvenes con el sistema educativo ante el nuevo pacto de inclusión en el nivel medio. In N. López, R. Opertti & C. Vargas Tamez (eds.), *Adolescentes y jóvenes en realidades cambiantes. Notas para repensar la educación secundaria en América Latina*. París: UNESCO, pp. 12–39.

de la Torre, A., Messina, J. & Silva, J. (2017). The inequality story in Latin America and the Caribbean: Searching for an explanation. In L. Bértola & J. Williamson (eds.), *Has Latin American Inequality Changed Direction? Looking Over the Long Run*. New York: Springer, pp. 317–38.

Di Cesare, M. (2011). *El perfil epidemiológico de América Latina y el Caribe: desafíos, límites y acciones*. Santiago de Chile: CEPAL.

Di Virgilio, M. M. & Perelman, M. (2014). Ciudades latinoamericanas. La producción social de las desigualdades urbanas. In M. M. Di Virgilio & M. Perelman (eds.), *Ciudades latinoamericanas: Desigualdad, segregación y tolerancia*. Buenos Aires: CLACSO, pp. 8–19.

Duarte, J., Gargiulo, C. & Moreno, M. (2012). Infraestructura escolar y aprendizajes en la educación básica latinoamericana: un análisis a partir del SERCE. In M. Cabrol & M. Székely (eds.), *Educación para la Transformación*. Washington, DC: Inter-American Development Bank, pp. 205–44.

Dubet, F. (2012). Los límites de la igualdad de oportunidades. *Nueva sociedad*, 239, pp. 42–50.

ECLAC (2002). *Social Panorama of Latin America*. Santiago de Chile: ECLAC.

ECLAC (2008). *Transformaciones demográficas y su influencia en el desarrollo en América Latina y el Caribe*. Santiago de Chile: ECLAC.

ECLAC (2012). *Población, territorio y desarrollo sostenible*. Santiago de Chile: ECLAC.

ECLAC (2013). *Mujeres indígenas en América Latina. Dinámicas demográficas y sociales en el marco de los derechos humanos*. Santiago de Chile: ECLAC.

ECLAC (2014a). *Demographic Observatory, 2013* (LC/G.2615-P). Santiago de Chile: ECLAC.

ECLAC (2014b). *Compacts for Equality: Towards a Sustainable Future*. Santiago de Chile: ECLAC.

ECLAC (2014c). *Guaranteeing Indigenous People's Rights in Latin America*. Santiago de Chile: ECLAC.

ECLAC (2015a). *Demographic Observatory, 2015* (LC/G.2675-P). Santiago de Chile: ECLAC.

ECLAC (2015b). *Latin America and the Caribbean: Looking Ahead after the Millennium Development Goals. Regional Monitoring Report on the*

Millennium Development Goals in Latin America and the Caribbean. Santiago de Chile: ECLAC.

ECLAC (2016). *Social Panorama of Latin America 2015.* Santiago de Chile: ECLAC.

ECLAC (2017). *Social Panorama of Latin America 2016.* Santiago de Chile: ECLAC.

ECLAC (2018). *Social Panorama of Latin America 2017.* Santiago de Chile: ECLAC.

Elacqua, G., Hincapié, D., Vegas E. & Alfonso, M. (2018). *Profesión: profesor en América Latina ¿Por qué se perdió el prestigio docente y cómo recuperarlo?* Washington, DC: Inter-American Development Bank.

Esteve, A. & Lesthaeghe, R. J. (eds.) (2016). *Cohabitation and Marriage in the Americas: Geo-historical Legacies and New Trends.* Berlin: Springer.

Feldman, D., Atorresi, A. & Mekler, V. (2013). Planes y programas para mejorar el aprendizaje y reducir el fracaso en la educación básica en América Latina. *Revista Latinoamericana de Educación Comparada*, 4 (4), 12–24.

Fernández, M. & Messina, J. (2017). *Skill Premium, Labor Supply, and Changes in the Structure of Wages in Latin America.* IDB Working Paper 786. Washington, DC: Inter-American Development Bank.

Fernandez-Cano, A. (2016). Una crítica metodológica de las evaluaciones PISA. *RELIEVE. Revista Electrónica de Investigación y Evaluación Educativa*, 22(1), 1–17.

Filgueira, F., Reygadas, L., Luna, J. P. & Alegre, P. (2012). Crisis de incorporación en América Latina: límites de la modernización conservadora. *Perfiles latinoamericanos*, 20(40), 7–34.

Galvão, L., Finkelman, J. & Henao, S. (2010). *Determinantes ambientales y sociales de la salud.* Washington, DC: PAHO.

Gasparini, L., Cruces, G. & Tornarolli, L. (2011). Recent trends in income inequality in Latin America. *Economía*, 10(Spring), 147–201.

Gasparini, L., Cruces, G. & Tornarolli, L. (2016). *Chronicle of a Deceleration Foretold: Income inequality in Latin America in the 2010s.* Documento de Trabajo 198. La Plata: CEDLAS-UNLP.

Gómez Sabaini, J. C., Jiménez, J.P. & Morán, D. (2017). El impacto fiscal de los recursos naturales no renovables. In J. C. Gómez Sabaini, J. P. Jiménez & R. Martner (eds.), *Consensos y conflictos en la política tributaria de América Latina* (LC/PUB. 2017/5-P). Santiago de Chile: CEPAL, pp. 393–414.

Gómez Sabaini, J. C. & Morán, D. (2017). El nivel y la estructura de la carga tributaria en los países de la región. In J. C. Gómez Sabaini, J. P. Jiménez &

R. Martner (eds.), *Consensos y conflictos en la política tributaria de América Latina* (LC/PUB. 2017/5-P). Santiago de Chile: CEPAL, pp. 35–66.

Guttmacher Institute (2018). *Aborto en América Latina y el Caribe: Hoja informativa*. New York: Guttmacher Institute.

Hanni, M., Martner, R. & Podestá, A. (2017). La incidencia distributiva de la fiscalidad en América Latina. In J. C. Gómez Sabaini, J. P. Jiménez & R. Martner (eds.), *Consensos y conflictos en la política tributaria de América Latina* (LC/PUB. 2017/5-P). Santiago: CEPAL, pp. 122–44.

Hanushek, E. & Woessmann, L. (2009). *Schooling, Cognitive Skills, and the Latin American Growth Puzzle*. Working Paper 15066. Cambridge, MA: NBER. http://scid.stanford.edu/system/files/shared/Hanushek_5-13-09 .pdf.

Hillis, S., Mercy J., Amobi A. & Kress, H. (2016). Global prevalence of past-year violence against children: A systematic review and minimum estimates. *Pediatrics*, 137(3). http://pediatrics.aappublications.org/content/ early/2016/01/25/peds.2015–4079.

Hoffman, K. & Centeno, M. A. (2003). The lopsided continent: Inequality in Latin America. *Annual Review of Sociology*, 29(1), 363–90.

Hoyos, R., Rogers, H. & Székely, M. (2016). *Ninis en América Latina: 20 millones de jóvenes en busca de oportunidades*. Washington, DC: Banco Mundial.

Huber, E. & Stephens, J. D. (2012). *Democracy and the Left: Social Policy and Inequality in Latin America*. Chicago, IL: University of Chicago Press.

Jiménez, J. P. (2017). Equidad y sistema tributario en América Latina. *Nueva Sociedad*, 272, 52–67.

Kuh, D. L. & Ben-Shlomo, Y. (1997). *A Life Course Approach to Chronic Disease Epidemiology: Tracing the Origins of Ill-health from Early to Adult Life*. Oxford: Oxford University Press.

Lattes, A. E., Rodríguez, J. & Villa, M. (2003). Population dynamics and urbanization in Latin America: Concepts and data limitations. In T. Champion & H. Graeme (comps.), *New Forms of Urbanization: Beyond the Urban-Rural Dichotomy*. Aldershot: Ashgate, pp. 89–111.

Laurell, A. C. (2016). Las reformas de salud en América Latina: procesos y resultados. *Cuadernos de Relaciones Laborales*, 34(2), 293–314.

Lee, R. & Mason, A. (2006). What is the demographic dividend? *Finance and Development*, 43(3), 16–17.

Levitsky, S. & Roberts, K. M. (eds.) (2011).*The Resurgence of the Latin American Left*. Baltimore: Johns Hopkins University Press.

Levy, S. & Schady, N. (2013). Latin America's social policy challenge: Education, social insurance, redistribution. *Journal of Economic Perspectives*, 27(2), 193–218.

Lloyd-Sherlock, P. (2000). Old age and poverty in developing countries: new policy challenges. *World Development*, 28(12), 2157–68.

Londoño, J. & Székely, M. (2000). Persistent poverty and excess inequality: Latin America, 1970–1995. *Journal of Applied Economics*, 3(1), 93–134.

López-Calva, L. F. & Ortiz-Juarez, E. (2014). A vulnerability approach to the definition of the middle class. *Journal of Economic Inequality*, 12(1), 23–47.

Lora, E (2007) "State Reform in Latin American. A silent Revolution in Lora, E. (ed.)The State of State Reform in Latin America, IADB, Washington.

Lora, E. & Fajardo, J. (2013). Latin American middle classes: The distance between perception and reality. *Economía*, 14(1), 33–54.

Lugo, M. T. & Brito, A. (2015). Las Políticas TIC en la educación de América Latina. Una oportunidad para saldar deudas pendientes. Archivos de Ciencias de la Educación. www.archivosdeciencias.fahce.unlp.edu.ar/article/view/Archivos09a03.

Lustig, N., López-Calva, L. F. & Ortiz-Juarez, E. (2011). *The Decline in Inequality in Latin America: How Much, Since When and Why*. Working Paper 1118. New Orleans, LA: Tulane University, Department of Economics.

Malgouyres, F. (2014). Descentralización y recentralización educativa en una perspectiva comparada de tres países federales latinoamericanos. *Trace [En línea]*, 65, 69–80.

Martín, E. (2011). Currículo y evaluación estandarizada: colaboración o tensión. In E. Martín & F. M. Rizo (Eds.). *Avances y desafíos en la evaluación educativa*. Buenos Aires: OEI-Fundación Santillana, pp. 88–98.

Martínez Pizarro, J. & Orrego Rivera, C. (2016). *Nuevas tendencias y dinámicas migratorias en América Latina y el Caribe*. Serie Población y Desarrollo 114. Santiago de Chile: CEPAL.

Maurizio, R. (2014). *El impacto distributivo del salario mínimo en la Argentina, el Brasil, Chile y el Uruguay*. Serie Políticas Sociales 194. Santiago de Chile: CEPAL.

Mauttone, A. & Hernández, D. (2017). *Encuesta de movilidad del área metropolitana de Montevideo. Principales resultados e indicadores*. Montevideo: CAF, Intendencia de Montevideo, Intendencia de Canelones, Intendencia de San José, Ministerio de Transporte y Obras Públicas, Universidad de la República, PNUD Uruguay. http://scioteca.caf.com/handle/123456789/1078.

Molina, C. & Tobar, F. (2018). ¿Qué significa Neoliberalismo en salud? *RevIISE: Revista de Ciencias Sociales y Humanas*, 12(12), 65–73.

Montero, L. & García, J. (2017). *Panorama multidimensional del desarrollo urbano en América Latina y el Caribe*. Santiago de Chile: CEPAL.

OECD (2014). *PISA 2012 Results: What Students Know and Can Do – Student Performance in Mathematics, Reading and Science (Volume I, Revised edition, February 2014)*. PISA, OECD Publishing. www.oecd.org/pisa/keyfind ings/pisa-2012-results-volume-I.pdf.

OREAL (2001). *Situación educativa de América Latina y el Caribe. 1980–2000*. Oficina Regional de Educación para América Latina y el Caribe. Santiago de Chile: UNESCO.

Oxfam (2015). *Privilegios que niegan derechos. Desigualdad extrema y secuestro de la democracia en América Latina y el Caribe*. Oxford: Oxfam International.

PAHO (2009). *Epidemiología de los trastornos mentales en América Latina y el Caribe*. Washington, DC: PAHO.

PAHO (2017). *Health in the Americas: Regional Outlook and Country Profiles*. Washington, DC: PAHO.

PAHO (2018a). *La carga de los trastornos mentales en la Región de las Américas*. Washington, DC: PAHO.

PAHO (2018b). *Just Societies: Health Equity and Dignified Lives. Executive Summary of the Report of the Commission of the Pan American Health Organization on Equity and Health Inequalities in the Americas*. Washington, DC: PAHO.

Pardo, I. & Varela, C. (2013). La fecundidad bajo el reemplazo y las políticas familiares en América Latina y el Caribe: qué puede aprenderse de la experiencia europea. *Revista Brasileira de Estudos de População*, 30(2), 503–18.

Raczynski, D., Wieinstein, J. & Pascual, J. (2013). Subvención escolar preferencial (SEP) en Chile: Un intento por equilibrar la macro y micro política escolar. *Revista Iberoamericana Sobre Calidad, Eficacia y Cambio en Educación*, 11, 164–93.

Rama, C. (2009). La tendencia a la masificación de la cobertura de la educación superior en América Latina. *Revista iberoamericana de educación*, 50, 173–95.

Rico, M. N. & Maldonado Valera, C. (2011). *Las familias latinoamericanas interrogadas. Hacia la articulación del diagnóstico, la legislación y las políticas*. Serie Seminarios y Conferencias 61. Santiago de Chile: ECLAC–UNFPA.

Rivas, A. & Sanchez, B. (2016). Políticas y resultados educativos en América Latina: un mapa comparado de siete países (2000–2015). *Relieve* 22(1), http://dx.doi.org/10.7203/relieve.22.1.8245.

Roberts, K. M. (2012). *The Politics of Inequality and Redistribution in Latin America's Post-adjustment Era*. WIDER Working Paper 2012/08. Helsinki: United Nations University, World Institute for Development Economics Research.

Robles, M., Rubio, M. G. & Stampini, M. (2015). *Have Cash Transfers Succeeded in Reaching the Poor in Latin America and the Caribbean?* Policy Brief 246. Washington, DC: Inter-American Development Bank.

Rodríguez Vignoli, J. (2002). *Distribución territorial de la población de América Latina y el Caribe: tendencias, interpretaciones y desafíos para las políticas públicas*. Serie Población y Desarrollo 32. Santiago de Chile: ECLAC.

Rodríguez Vignoli, J. (2011). *Migración interna y sistema de ciudades en América Latina: intensidad, patrones, efectos y potenciales determinantes, censos de la década del 2000*. Serie Población y Desarrollo 105. Santiago de Chile: ECLAC.

Rodríguez Vignoli, J. (2014). Fecundidad adolescente en América Latina. Una actualización. In S. Cavenaghi & W. Cabella (eds.), *Comportamiento reproductivo y fecundidad en América Latina: una agenda inconclusa*. Río de Janeiro: ALAP, pp. 33–65.

Rodríguez Vignoli, J., Di Cesare, M. & Páez, K. (2017). *Reproducción temprana: diferencias entre grandes regiones del mundo al inicio y al final de la adolescencia*. Serie Población y Desarrollo 117. Santiago de Chile: ECLAC.

Rozas, P. (2010). Latin America: Problems and challenges of infrastructure financing. *CEPAL Review*, 101, 59–82.

Ruprah, I. N. (2010). *Does Owning Your Home Make You Happier? Impact Evidence from Latin America*. Working Paper OVE/WP-02-10. Washington, DC: Inter-American Development Bank.

Salazar-Xirinachs, J. M. & Chacaltana, J. (2018). La informalidad en América Latina y el Caribe: ¿Por qué persiste y cómo superarla? In J. M. Salazar-Xirinachs & J. Chacaltana (eds.), *Políticas de formalización en América Latina. Avances y desafíos*. Lima: OIT, Oficina Regional para América Latina y el Caribe, pp. 13–47.

SITEAL (2015a). *Resumen estadístico comentado. Escolarización e Infancia América Latina, 2000–2013*. Buenos Aires: IIPE-UNESCO.

SITEAL (2015b). *Resumen estadístico comentado. Escolarización y Adolescencia, América Latina, 2000–2013*. Buenos Aires: IIPE-UNESCO.

SITEAL (2016). *Escolarización y Juventud. América Latina, 2000 – 2013*. Buenos Aires: IIPE-UNESCO.

Soares, S., Guerreiro Osório, R., Veras Soares, F., Medeiros, M. & Zepeda, E. (2009). Conditional cash transfers in Brazil, Chile and Mexico: Impacts upon inequality. *Estudios Económicos*, special issue (February), 207–24.

Spijker, J., López Ruiz, L. & Esteve Palós, A. (2012). Tres décadas de cambio y continuidad en la nupcialidad latinoamericana. *Notas de población*, 94, 11–36.

Tavares de Almeida, M. H. (2017). Brasil: capas medias, protesta y agenda pública. In L. Paramio & C. Güemes (eds.), *Las nuevas clases medias latinoamericanas: ascenso e incertidumbre*. Madrid: Centro de Estudios Políticos y Constitucionales, pp. 113–32.

Tedesco, J. C. (2012). *Educación y justicia social en América Latina*. Buenos Aires: Fondo de Cultura Económica.

Tobar, F., Drago, M. T. B., Hamilton, G., Lifschitz, E. & Yjilioff, R. D. (2014). *Respuestas a las enfermedades catastróficas*. Buenos Aires: CIPPEC. www .cippec.org/wp-content/uploads/2017/03/1283.pdf.

Ullmann, H., Maldonado Valera, C. & Rico, M. N. (2014). *La evolución de las estructuras familiares en América Latina, 1990–2010: Los retos de la pobreza, la vulnerabilidad y el cuidado*. Serie Políticas Sociales 193. Santiago de Chile: ECLAC.

UN DESA (2018). *World Urbanization Prospects: The 2018 Revision*, online edn. New York: Population Division, UN DESA.

UN DESA (2019). *World Population Prospects 2019*, online edn., rev. 1. New York: Population Division, UN DESA.

UN-Habitat (2012). *State of Latin American and Caribbean Cities 2012: Towards a New Urban Transition*. Nairobi: UN-Habitat.

UNICEF (2009). *Atlas sociolingüístico de pueblos indígenas de América Latina*. La Paz: UNICEF-FUNPROEIB.

UNICEF (2016). *Informe sobre Equidad en Salud: Un análisis de las inequidades en salud reproductiva, materna, neonatal, de la niñez y de la adolescencia en América Latina y el Caribe para guiar la formulación de políticas*. Panama: UNICEF.

UN Women (2017). *El progreso de las mujeres en América Latina y el Caribe 2017. Transformar la economía para realizar los derechos*. Panama: UN Women.

Uribe, M. C. & Bejarano, J. C. (2009). *A Policy Guide to Rental Housing in Developing Countries: Quick Policy Guide Series*, vol. 1. Nairobi: UN-Habitat.

Urriola, C., Infante, A., Aguilera, I. & Ormeño, H. (2016). La reforma de salud chilena a diez años de su implementación. *Salud Pública de México*, 58(5), 514–21.

Vidal, J. & Di Fabio, J. L. Judicialización y acceso a tecnologías sanitarias: oportunidades y riesgos. *Rev Panam Salud Pública*. 2017;41:e137. doi: 10.26633/RPSP.2017.137.

Ward, P., Jiménez, J. & Di Virgilio, M. M. (2014). Extensive case study methodology for the analysis of self-help housing consolidation, household organization and family mobility. *Current Urban Studies*, 2, 83–162.

Weller, J. (comp.) (2017). *Empleo en América Latina y el Caribe. Textos seleccionados 2006–2017*. Santiago de Chile: CEPAL.

WHO (2000). *A Life Course Approach to Health*. Geneva: WHO.

WHO (2013). *Global and Regional Estimates of Violence against Women: Prevalence and Health Effects of Intimate Partner Violence and Non-partner Sexual Violence*. Geneva: WHO.

World Bank (2018). *Afro-descendants in Latin America: Toward a Framework of Inclusion*. Washington, DC: World Bank.

Cambridge Elements ⁼

Elements in Politics and Society in Latin America

Maria Victoria Murillo
Columbia University

Maria Victoria Murillo is Professor of Political Science and International Affairs at Columbia University. She is the author of *Political Competition, Partisanship, and Policymaking in the Reform of Latin American Public Utilities* (Cambridge, 2009). She is also editor of *Carreras Magisteriales, Desempeño Educativo y Sindicatos de Maestros en América Latina* (2003), and co-editor of *Argentine Democracy: the Politics of Institutional Weakness* (2005). She has published in edited volumes as well as in the *American Journal of Political Science, World Politics, Comparative Political Studies* among others.

Juan Pablo Luna
The Pontifical Catholic University of Chile

Juan Pablo Luna is Professor in the Department of Political Science at The Pontifical Catholic University of Chile. He is the author of *Segmented Representation. Political Party Strategies in Unequal Democracies*, and has co-authored *Latin American Party Systems* (Cambridge, 2010). His work on political representation, state capacity, and organized crime has appeared in *Comparative Political Studies, Revista de Ciencia Política*, the *Journal of Latin American Studies, Latin American Politics and Society, Studies in Comparative International Development* among others.

Tulia G. Falleti
University of Pennsylvania

Tulia G. Falleti is the Class of 1965 Term Associate Professor of Political Science, Director of the Latin American and Latino Studies Program, and Senior Fellow of the Leonard Davis Institute for Health Economics at the University of Pennsylvania. She is the author of the award-winning Decentralization and Subnational Politics in Latin America (Cambridge, 2010). She is co-editor of *The Oxford Handbook of Historical Institutionalism*, among other edited books. Her articles have appeared in many edited volumes and journals such as the *American Political Science Review and Comparative Political Studies*.

Andrew Schrank
Brown University

Andrew Schrank is the Olive C. Watson Professor of Sociology and International & Public Affairs at Brown University. His articles on business, labor, and the state in Latin America have appeared in the *American Journal of Sociology, Comparative Politics, Comparative Political Studies, Latin American Politics & Society, Social Forces*, and *World Development*, among other journals, and his co-authored book, *Root-Cause Regulation: Labor Inspection in Europe and the Americas*, is out soon.

About the Series

Latin American politics and society are at a crossroads, simultaneously confronting serious challenges and remarkable opportunities that are likely to be shaped by formal institutions and informal practices alike. The new Politics and Society in Latin America Cambridge Elements series will offer multidisciplinary and methodologically pluralist contributions on the most important topics and problems confronted by the region.

Cambridge Elements ☰

Elements in Politics and Society in Latin America

Elements in the Series

Understanding Institutional Weakness: Power and Design in Latin American Institutions
Daniel M. Brinks, Steven Levitsky and Maria Victoria Murillo

A full series listing is available at: www.cambridge.org/PSLT

CPSIA information can be obtained
at www.ICGtesting.com
Printed in the USA
LVHW112136040220
645827LV00010B/1424